If you think my preaching's bad,

TRY MY JOKES

David Pytches

D1324750

MONARCH
BOOKS
Oxford, UK

Published by Monarch Books
an imprint of
Lion Hudson plc
Wilkinson House, Jordan Hill Road,
Oxford OX2 8DR, England
Email: monarch@lionhudson.com
www.lionhudson.com/monarch

ISBN: 978-1-85424-868-8
e-ISBN 978-0-85721-400-3

First edition 2008

Acknowledgments
Unless otherwise stated, Scripture quotations are
taken from the Holy Bible, New International Version,
© 1973, 1978, 1984 by the International Bible Society.
Used by permission of Hodder and Stoughton Ltd.
All rights reserved.

A catalogue record for this book is available
from the British Library

Contents

Introduction

With mirth and laughter let old wrinkles come.
William Shakespeare

The wise old King Solomon tells us that there is a time to laugh and a time to weep (Ecclesiastes 3:4).

Laughing counters toxic tensions, lightens dark moods and defuses difficult situations. Laughter releases healing endorphins. *The Sunday Telegraph* columnist Sandi Toksvig wrote recently, tongue in cheek: 'Personally I think jokes should be available on the National Health Service.' Humour serves so many good purposes.

Matters of social concern can be playfully confronted through joking. Cartoons can highlight our foibles and lampoon our blind spots in fun. In most families, communities and races, light-hearted ribbing smoothes ruffled feathers and strengthens affections. It actually makes people feel included when they are the centre of attention through gentle teasing.

Of course, humour can be misused, but it is a pity that it is considered politically incorrect to joke about some of our racial differences, language problems, cultural misunderstandings and even some of our religious pretensions. Jokes can highlight potential problems and enable us to make sensitive adjustments without wounding personal feelings. Laughter sugars the pill for swallowing good doses of wisdom. An ancient Jewish proverb explains the process so well: 'A merry heart doeth good like a medicine' (Proverbs 17:22).

Jokes arise from real-life situations and cover a whole range of human emotions, sensitivities and activities. A funny element in many jokes is that of an unexpected connection between names or people in a given situation, or opinions quoted out of context, or the risk of mild shock in sedate company. 'The essence of humour is surprise; that is why you laugh when you see a joke in *Punch*' (A. P. Herbert).

I believe the contents of this book are free from words or subjects that would profoundly offend or cause any real distress. This does not mean that all sensitive topics have been automatically excluded. We must surely agree that there are ludicrous sides to sex as there are to marriage, child-rearing or whatever. But I don't think any jokes on any subject here would be considered offensive when used appropriately. Obviously, any joke can be ill-suited to some situations – for example, jokes about death at a funeral.

After quotations, the names of those who are believed to be their originators appear in brackets.

I want to acknowledge my debt to the following: Ricky Feuille, John Coles, Mark Bailey, Mark Melluish, John Hughes, Len Spencer and Jordon Wright for some of the offerings included here, since they kindly sent their selections of jokes to me. Their initials follow their particular contributions. 'If their humour is not appreciated their nerve must surely be admired' (with apologies to Oscar Wilde).

David Pytches

Warm-up Quips, Quotes and Jokes

Good practice

Whenever anything bad happens to me, I write a joke about it. Then it's no longer a bad experience. It's a tax deduction! (Denise Munro)

....

The cost of a free lunch

Every rose has its thorn –
That's the catch life teaches.
There has not been a free lunch yet
Without those long boring speeches.

....

Spinning it out

Years ago John Timpson used to run the *Today* programme on Radio 4 with Brian Redhead. I once heard him tell how, as a young reporter, he began work with the *East Anglian Daily Times*. He went on to become a reporter, and was once detailed by the BBC to sail with the Royals on *Britannia*. He described how one day he actually came face to face with the Duke of Edinburgh at the foot of a gangway. A quick cross-examination ensued:

'Hello! Who are you?'

'Timpson, sir!'

'And what are you doing here?'

'I'm working for the BBC as no. 2 on the Royals.'

'Oh!'

'And that was the end of the conversation,' Timpson later recalled, but maximizing on the briefest of encounters, he added: 'However, I always felt it came from the heart!'

....

Forecast

Widespread fist and mog
can be expected.

(Weather bloomer)

....

A whole gallery

Everyone has heard of the Tate family. They are everywhere. There is Dick Tate, who wants to control everybody. Ro Tate wants to turn things around. Agi Tate stirs things up and Irri Tate lends an intrusive hand. Hesi Tate and Vege Tate always procrastinate. Imi Tate mimics everybody. Devas Tate likes to destroy things and Poten Tate wants to be a big shot. But it's Facili Tate, Cogi Tate and Medi Tate who save the day for us.

(George Coote)

Deserved

If lawyers are disbarred and clergymen defrocked, doesn't it follow that electricians can be delighted, musicians denoted and disbanded, cowboys deranged, models deposed, teachers declassified, authors described, and doctors deciphered, while laundry workers can decrease, eventually becoming depressed and depleted? Gardeners can be defenced, dictionary compilers demeaned and train-operators departed. Even more, bed-makers will be debunked, baseball players debased, and equestrians derided.

Landscapers will be deflowered, bulldozer operators will be degraded, organ donors will be delivered, software engineers will be detested, and even musical composers will eventually decompose.

On a more positive note, though, perhaps we can hope that politicians will be devoted and decanted.

A good impression

On the young man's first date out with his girl-friend he decided to impress her. He took her to a high-class restaurant and ordered the whole meal in French. Even the waiter was surprised.

So was he, when it turned out to be a Chinese restaurant.

Blessed originality

Sometimes I wish I were Adam.
Whatever problems he may have had in
  days of yore,
When he cracked a joke no one could say,
'I've heard that one before.'

Low view

Everywhere I go, I'm asked if the universities stifle writers. My opinion is that they don't stifle enough of them.   (Flannery O'Connor)

Youth

I'm all for the young taking over, and thank God I won't be there when they do.   (Arthur Treacher)

Misers

Misers may not be very much fun to live with, but they make excellent ancestors.   (Ron Detinger)

A good fit

A man has his clothes made to fit him. A woman makes herself fit the clothes.   (Edgar Watson How)

....
Bridges and buttons

Men build bridges and stretch railroads across deserts, yet seem incapable of sewing on a button. (Heywood Broun)

....
Luck

With my luck, by the time I build a better mousetrap, mice will be an endangered species.

(Al Berstein)

Politics, Political Correctness and Diplomacy

Politics made simple

- *Capitalism:* You possess two cows. You sell one and buy a bull.
- *Socialism:* You possess two cows. You give one of them to your neighbour.
- *Communism:* You possess two cows. The government confiscates them and provides you with milk.
- *Nazism:* You possess two cows. The government confiscates them and shoots you.
- *The European Union:* You possess two cows. The government confiscates them, shoots one, milks the other and pours it down the drain.

....

A definition

A bulldozer is someone who sleeps through a political speech.

My chair

The former Australian Prime Minister, Bob Hawke, died and went to heaven.

As he approached the Lord enthroned, God said to him: 'Who are you?'

'I'm Bob Hawke. That's my chair you're sitting on.'

No help needed

Jim Hacker (played by the actor Paul Eddington): 'Humphrey, do you see it as part of your job to help ministers make fools of themselves?'

Sir Humphrey Appleby (Nigel Hawthorne): 'Well, I never met one who needed any help.'

(Yes, Minister)

Hot air

He had listened to the politician's speech for a solid hour before going outside for a breath of fresh air.

'Is he still talking?' asked a mate outside.

'Yeah.'

'What's he talking about?'

'He didn't say.'

Fanatic

A fanatic is someone who is sure the Almighty would agree with him, if only the Almighty had all the background information. (Robert E. Harris)

Noble deed

Late one night the Prime Minister was walking by the riverside preoccupied by the affairs of state. He suddenly slipped and fell in the water. A young man heard his cries for help and, at great personal risk, dived in and saved him.

As he recovered the Prime Minister said to the young man: 'Thank you – you saved my life! Anything you name, you can have.'

'I don't want anything,' said the young man. 'Just don't tell my Dad.'

Summing up

My opponent has a problem. He won't get elected unless things get worse – and things won't get worse unless he's elected. (George Bush)

Compromise

Compromise is the art of dividing a cake so that everybody thinks he is getting the largest piece.

A new political party

A crocodile wanted to form a new political party. He approached an elephant and asked, 'Mr Elephant, would you join my new political party?'

'Oh, I'm so sorry, I can't,' said the elephant. 'You see, our family are just not made for that kind of thing. I just step all over people, my wife steps all over people and our children step all over people.'

Disappointed, the crocodile continued on his way and met a giraffe.

'Ah! Mr Giraffe, would you like to join my new political party?'

The giraffe thought about it and then refused: 'Oh, I'm so sorry, but it would be counter-productive,' he said. 'You see, I look down on everyone, my wife looks down on everyone and our children look down on everyone.'

The ever-hopeful crocodile moved on and met Mr Bear. 'Ah! Mr Bear, won't you join my new political party?'

'No,' said the bear. 'I'm afraid it would be most unsuitable. I wear a fur coat, my wife wears a fur coat, and our children all wear fur coats. But tell me, Mr Crocodile, why ever do you want to form a political party?'

'Well, you see,' the crocodile replied, 'I have a big mouth, my wife has a big mouth and our children all have big mouths!'   (L.S.)

Not to be encouraged

Don't vote for politicians.
It just encourages them.

(Billy Connolly)

The art of government

Q. Why is the House of Commons like a Picasso painting?

A. Eyes to the right, nose to the left!

Political acrobatics

The politician is an acrobat; he keeps his balance by doing the opposite of what he says.

(Maurice Barres)

Circling for blood

There are no true friends in politics. We are all sharks circling, and waiting, for traces of blood to appear in the water. (Alan Clark)

The media

Politicians who complain about the media are like ships' captains who complain about the sea.

(Enoch Powell)

Most promising

Vote for the man who promises least; he'll be the least disappointing. (Bernard Baruch)

Tactful words

Q. What is the difference between a diplomat and a lady?

A. When a diplomat says 'yes', he means 'perhaps'. When he says 'perhaps', he means 'no'. When he says 'no', he is not a diplomat. When a lady says 'no', she means 'perhaps'. When she says 'perhaps', she means 'yes'. But if she says 'yes', she is no lady.

A cultivated skill

Etiquette is knowing how to yawn with your mouth closed.

Incomes policy

The government's incomes policy is as significant as a blush on a dead man's cheek.

(Clive Jenkins)

Four Hittites

A politician was constantly in trouble for telling politically incorrect jokes. He decided that in future he would tell all his racist jokes about the Hittites – an extinct race. The next time he told a joke, he began: 'There were these four Hittites – Tommy, Taffy, Murphy and Jock…'

A barren spouse

Three Hittites were discussing their children. One professed to having no children, explaining that his wife was 'inconceivable'.

'No! no! no!' said the second man. 'You don't mean your wife is inconceivable – you mean she is *impregnable*.'

'That's not right either,' said the third man. 'He means his wife is *unbearable*.'

Desert island

A shipful of people from the British Isles was washed up on a desert island. It was nearly a year before the survivors could be picked up. By that time the Scots had started a brewery, the Welsh had started a choir, the Irish were on the beach fighting, while the English were still waiting for an introduction!

Mutual benefit

When a reporter asked a former Prime Minister of New Zealand, David Lange, if he was concerned about the exodus of so many New Zealanders to Australia, the ex-PM responded, 'Not at all. I think it's bound to raise the IQ of both countries.'

A lesson from Columbus

When Columbus started out, he didn't know where he was going. When he got there, he didn't know where he was. When he got back, he didn't know where he had been. And he did it all on other people's money. What a politician!

Unprepared

Politics is perhaps the only profession for which no preparation is thought necessary.

(Robert Louis Stevenson)

Looking up

It's very difficult to look up to a leader who is trying to keep his ear to the ground.

Diplomacy

A diplomat is a person who can tell you to go to hell in such a way that you actually look forward to the trip. (Caskie Stinnet)

Diplomacy is the art of saying things in such a way that nobody knows exactly what you mean.

A definition of diplomacy: *Lying in state.*

Refugees

People who vote with their feet.

Ignorance

I do not believe in the collective wisdom of individual ignorance. (Thomas Carlyle)

Placating the enemy

An infallible method of conciliating a tiger is to allow oneself to be devoured.

Good advice

The most distinctive mark of a cultured mind is the ability to take another's point of view; to put oneself in another's place, and see life and its problems from a point of view different from one's own. To be willing to test a new idea; to be able to live on the edge of difference in all matters intellectually; to examine without heat the burning questions of the day, to have imaginative sympathy, openness and flexibility of mind, steadiness and poise of feeling, cool calmness of judgement, is to have culture. (A. H. R. Fairchild)

Preferred place for retirement

I would like to live in Manchester, England. The transition between Manchester and death would be unnoticeable.   (Mark Twain)

Sex on the brain

The English have sex on the brain – which is a frightfully uncomfortable place to have it.

(Malcolm Muggeridge)

Mafia morality

We must keep America whole and safe and unspoiled.

(Al Capone)

Hand-picked

The high standards of Australians are due to the fact that their ancestors were all hand-picked by the best English judges.   (Douglas Copland)

Just a joke, Jock

The Irish gave the bagpipes to the Scots as a joke, but the Scots haven't seen the joke yet.

(Oliver Herford)

No hurry

There are over thirty words in the Irish language which are equivalent to the Spanish *mañana*. But somehow none of them conveys the same sense of urgency.   (Patrick Kavanagh)

The ultimate cure

The French invented the only known cure for dandruff. It is called the guillotine.   (P. G. Wodehouse)

Measuring success

We had a very successful trip to Russia – we got back.

(Bob Hope)

A different culture

A gesticulation is any movement made by a foreigner.

(J. B. Morton)

A laudable ambition

What do I think of Western civilization? I think it would be a very good idea.   (Mahatma Gandhi)

Unprintable

When asked his opinion of Welsh nationalism, Mr Thomas replied in three words, two of which were 'Welsh nationalism'.   (Dylan Thomas)

Terrorism alert

The USA has become so tense and nervous. It's been years since I've seen anyone asleep in church.

(Norman Vincent Peale)

A strange conclusion

In Italy for thirty years under the Borgias they had warfare, terror, murder, bloodshed, but they produced Michelangelo, Leonardo da Vinci, and the Renaissance. In Switzerland, they had brotherly love, they had five hundred years of democracy and peace. And what did they produce? The cuckoo-clock. (Orson Wells)

Pure prejudice

I can never forgive God for creating the French.

(Peter Ustinov)

Vive la France!

The English love France. They just wish the French didn't live there.

Advice to foreigners

On entering an English railway carriage it is customary to shake hands with all the passengers.

(R. J. Phillips)

Is that so?

The devil will not come to Cornwall, for fear of being put into a pie.   (Clement Freud)

English superiority

The world still consists of two clearly divided groups; the English and foreigners. One group consists of less than 50 million people; the other of 3,950 million. The latter group doesn't really count.

(George Mikes)

Committees

A committee is a group of people who individually can do nothing, but together decide that nothing can be done.   (Fred Allen)

If Moses had been a committee, the Israelites would still be in Egypt.

A committee is a group of the unwilling, picked from the unfit, to do the unnecessary.

(Richard Harkness)

Walter Mondale

He has all the charisma of
a speed bump.

(Will Durst)

Aneurin Bevan

He was the only man I knew who could make a
curse sound like a caress. (Michael Foot)

Tony Benn

He immatures with age.

(Harold Wilson)

After Harold Macmillan's 1962 cabinet purge

Greater love hath no man than this, that he lay
down his friends for his life. (Jeremy Thorpe)

Clement Attlee

He reminds me of nothing so much as a dead fish
before it has had time to stiffen. (George Orwell)

Anthony Eden

He is forever poised between a cliché and an indiscretion. (Harold Macmillan)

Clement Attlee

He is a sheep in sheep's clothing.
(Winston Churchill)

Stanley Baldwin

He occasionally stumbles over the truth but he always hastily picks himself up and hurries on as if nothing had happened. (Winston Churchill)

Stanley Baldwin! One could not even dignify him with the name of stuffed shirt. He was simply a hole in the air. (George Orwell)

Stafford Cripps

Stafford Cripps has a first-rate mind until he makes it up.
(Violet Asquith)

David Lloyd George

He spoke for a hundred and seventeen minutes, in which period he was detected only once in the use of an argument. (Arnold Bennett)

Charles De Gaulle

He looked like a female llama surprised in her bath.
(Winston Churchill)

Margaret Thatcher

I am thoroughly in favour of Mrs Thatcher's visit to the Falklands. I find a bit of hesitation, though, about her coming back. (John Mortimer)

Conditional patience

I am extraordinarily patient, provided I get my own way in the end. (Margaret Thatcher)

Weak arguments

One could drive a prairie schooner through any part of the arguments of William Jennings Bryan and never scrape against a fact. (David Huston)

Speechless

If the word 'No' was removed from the English language, Ian Paisley would be speechless.

(John Hume)

Sheep

The League of Nations is like sheep passing resolutions in favour of vegetarianism.   (Dean Inge)

Marriage and Home

Ignorance is bliss

A man may be a fool and not know it, but not if he is married.

(H. L. Mencken)

Heavy responsibility

Signing the register at a wedding, the best man had difficulty in making his ball-point pen work. 'Put your weight on it,' said the vicar, helpfully. The best man duly signed: *John Smith (ten stone, four pounds).*

Who decides?

In my house, I make all the major decisions and my wife makes the minor ones. For example, I decide about such things as East–West trade, crime in the streets, welfare cheating, and increases in taxes. My wife decides the minor things such as which house to buy, what kind of car we drive, how to spend the household budget, and how to raise the children.

Crazy

'Does everybody in your family suffer from insanity?'

'No, not at all, not at all. In fact we enjoy it!'

Thrown away

The average amount of time between throwing something away and needing it urgently is about two weeks. (Norman Bell)

Do dreams come true?

A woman told her husband of a dream she had just had in which he gave her a pearl necklace for Valentine's Day.

'What do you think it means?' she asked.

'You'll know tonight,' he assured her.

That evening he came home with a package which he gave to his wife. Delighted, she opened it – to find a book entitled *The Meaning of Dreams*.

The natural thing to do

To err is human; to blame it onto someone else is even more human.

(John Nadeau)

Happy memories

Remember that your wife is a romantic and still enjoys chocolates and flowers. So show her that you too remember, by talking about them now and then.

Newly married couple, at dinner

Wife, proudly: 'The two best things I cook are meat-loaf and apple dumplings.'

Husband, politely: 'Um…and which one is this?'

Cross-examination

Sympathetic Judge: 'Have you ever been cross-examined before?'

Witness: 'Yes your honour, I'm a married man.'

Snoring

There was a discussion in the press about the deleterious impact of snoring on the average marriage relationship. A third of the couples interviewed reckoned that it had definitely had a harmful effect on their love-making. The correspondence was closed after one reader wrote to suggest that the best solution would be for couples to do their love-making whilst they were awake.

Bravery

A wife nudged her husband awake when she thought she heard a burglar, but he refused to get out of bed to investigate.

'What happened?' she whispered angrily. 'You were *brave* when you married me.'

'Yes,' he replied. 'That's what my mates all said.'

What the future holds

The old couple sat on the porch, as they had for many years. 'I was just thinking,' said the old lady, 'we've had such a grand life together, but sooner or later one of us will pass on.'

'Yes, but don't worry about that now,' he said.

'Well, I was just thinking,' she replied, 'when that happens I'd like to go and live in Queensland.'

Spilling the beans

Two former neighbours bumped into each other after a long time and were having a good gossip over a cup of tea.

'And how are things going with you?' asked one.

'Oh,' said the other, 'I'm managing OK, although I lost my husband several months back.'

'I'm so sorry! How did that happen?'

'Well,' the other explained, 'I was making dinner and asked him to go out to the garden and pick some beans. After he had been gone some time I went out to see what the trouble was. And there he was dead – a heart attack!'

'How awful! What ever did you do?'

'Oh, I had a can of beans in the house and just used that.'

Zip, Zip, Zip!

A wife damaged her shoulder in a fall and thereafter could never manage to zip up her dresses. She would summon her husband at the appropriate moment and ask him to do it for her.

This became a daily routine. She would call him. He would come and zip it up with the words 'Zip, Zip, Zip! There you are, darling!'

And giving her a quick peck on the cheek he would dash off to work. Inwardly she felt a little miffed that he was not taking her ongoing handicap quite sympathetically enough.

One Saturday afternoon she was returning to her house. As she passed the car in the driveway she saw her husband tucked halfway under the car trying to adjust some part of the engine. Since his legs were protruding into the pathway, she bent down as she passed and pulled the zip on his jeans down and up – 'Zip, zip, zip!' She patted him on the thigh and said, 'There you are, darling! – Wasn't that a treat?'

Straightening up, she made for the back door, feeling rather smug, and entered her kitchen, only to find her husband putting on the kettle.

Think twice

The maximum penalty for bigamy:
two mothers-in-law.

Can't remember

George: 'Why don't Jack and Laura make up?'
Kate: 'They'd like to. Unfortunately they can't remember what they quarrelled about.'

Counselling

Marriage counsellor, to wife: 'Maybe your problem is that you've been waking up grumpy in the morning.'
Wife: 'No, I always let him sleep.'

His secret

Some people have asked the secret of our long marriage, and I explain:

'We take time to go to a restaurant twice a week and arrange a little candlelit dinner, with soft music, and a slow walk home. She goes Tuesdays; I go Fridays.'

Trouser trouble

The young wife was struggling to iron her husband's trousers.

'Forget it,' consoled her husband when she confessed. 'Remember, I've got an extra pair of trousers for that suit.'

'Yes, and it's lucky you have,' said she, drying her eyes. 'I used them to patch the hole.'

Working it out

She: 'I had to marry you to find out how stupid you are.'

He: 'You should have known the minute I asked you.'

Guess who?

A couple, just married, got two tickets to a very fine show as wedding presents. There was a handwritten note on the tickets reading, 'Guess who?'

They had no idea, but off they went to the play. When they returned, all their other wedding presents were gone. A note on the kitchen table said: 'Now you know!'

We were young

Wife: 'When we were younger, you used to nibble on my ear... Where are you going?'

Husband: 'To get my teeth!'

A good tip

To keep your marriage brimming
With love in the loving cup,
If ever you're wrong, admit it,
If ever you're right, shut up.

(Ogden Nash)

Females to the fore

Where the warfare is the hottest
In the battlefields of life,
You'll find the Christian soldier
Represented by his wife.

Traditional ideas

A vicar was experimenting in the village church with a new order of wedding service.

A local farmer was getting married, and on the day he was all dressed up to go to the wedding, when suddenly a message came through that one of his cows had escaped from a field.

Hurriedly he rolled up his trousers, kicked off his polished shoes and pulled on his wellies. Out he went to recapture the cow and get it back into a safe enclosure.

Arriving back rather breathless, he hastily donned his shoes but forgot to roll down his trouser legs.

As he arrived at the church the vicar greeted him, and in a whisper told him to pull his trousers down. The farmer stared back blankly.

So the vicar repeated his words, 'Pull your trousers down!'

'Look 'ere, Vicar,' the farmer replied. 'Oi hen't never been too 'appy about these 'ere modern sarvices. Oi think, arter orl, Oi'd rather we used the ole version.'

Talking to herself

Man: 'My wife is talking to herself quite a lot these days.'

Friend: 'My wife has been talking to herself for years, but has no idea. She thinks I'm listening.'

Hiccups

A man rushes into a chemist shop:

'Quick, what can you do for hiccups?'

The chemist leans across the counter and slaps him round the face.

'You fool! What did you do that for?'

'Well, it cured your hiccups.'

'Idiot! I wanted it for my wife in the car outside!'

Three wives

'Did you hear about the man who had three wives in three months? The first two died of poisoned mushrooms.'

'What happened to the third wife?'

'She died from strangling. She wouldn't eat the mushrooms!'

Toast

'Here's to you, darling.
No matter how old you are,
you don't look it.'

Why marry?

'I married my wife for her looks – but not the ones she has been giving me recently!'

The value of a wife

I did not marry my wife because she had four million. I would have married her if she only had two million. (Charles Forte)

Domestic interrogation

Webster is said to have been spurred on to write his first dictionary because every time he opened his mouth his nagging wife would say: 'And what's that supposed to mean?'

Miss Right

My parents made me promise to marry Miss Right. I was careful to do just that, but I never realized that one of her first names would be 'Always'!

A simple explanation

The teenage daughter got home very late and explained to her mother:

'You know how it is, Mum...'

'Yes, I certainly do. And what's his name?'

A bright home

'They say that children brighten the home.'

'They certainly do. They never turn the lights off.'

The man from Peru

There was an old man from Peru,
Who dreamt he was eating his shoe.
He woke in the night
In a terrible fright,
And found it was perfectly true.

Good to know you

Help a man in trouble and he'll never forget you –
especially next time he's in trouble. (Johnny Lyons)

A source of trouble

I have had more trouble with D. L. Moody than
with any other man I ever met.   (D. L. Moody)

Puzzling indeed

One morning I shot an elephant in my pyjamas.
How he got into my pyjamas I'll never know.

(Groucho Marx)

Reserved for later

The family had gathered around the bed where
their old grandfather lay dying.

'Is there anything I can do for you?' said his
wife tenderly.

The old man looked around and saw a large jug of beer on the table.

'I wouldn't mind a swig of that,' he croaked.

'Well, you can't!' snapped his wife. 'That's for the wake.'

Home sweet home

A mother was doing her best to look as if she was really enjoying the surprise birthday cake her little girl had baked and iced for her.

Seeing her mother's 'pleasure' as she struggled to swallow despite the strange taste and texture, the daughter said, 'I'm so glad you like it, Mummy. There should have been thirty-two candles on the cake, but they were all gone when I took it out of the oven.'

Women and Mothers

Lovely eyes

My wife has lovely coloured eyes. I particularly like the blue one.   (Bob Monkhouse)

....
Now we know

'How was it that you were born in Scunthorpe?'

   'Well, you see, I thought it was important to be near my mother.'

....
Bravo

There were eleven people hanging onto a rope beneath a helicopter – ten men and one woman.

   They all decided that one of them should let go because the rope would not carry their combined weight. If it were to break, all of them would fall to a certain death.

   No one could decide who should let go, so finally the woman gave a really moving speech, saying that she would gladly give up her life for them, as women were used to sacrificing themselves for others. They did it all the time for their husbands, their children and by giving in to men.

When she had finished speaking, all the men started clapping. (J.C.)

We know the feeling

Watching your daughter being collected by her date feels like handing over a million-dollar Stradivarius to a gorilla. (Jim Bishop)

Unpredictable

Any astronomer can predict with absolute accuracy just where every star in the universe will be at 11.30 tonight. He can make no such prediction about his teenage daughter. (James T. Adams)

What a bind

I hate housework! You make the beds, you do the dishes – and six months later you have to start all over again. (Joan Rivers)

A lucky find

A man is walking along a beach in California and finds a bottle. He picks it up and opens it. A genie suddenly appears from it and says, 'Thank you so much for letting me out after all those years. I must reward you. I can grant you just one wish.'

The man thinks and says, 'I have always wanted to go to Hawaii, but I can't because I have a phobia about flying and ships make me really sick. I would love it if you would build a bridge from here to Hawaii.'

The genie slowly shakes his head. 'That's too much. Just think of all the work involved – the huge pilings we'd need to hold up that highway, and the depths we would have to go to in order to reach the bottom of the ocean. Then there's all the cement. Also, with the distance involved, we would need petrol stations and rest stops along the way. It really is a bit too much to ask. But I'd still love to help you. Can't you think of anything else?'

The man thinks and says, 'Well! There is one thing I've always wanted to know. I'd really like to be able to understand women. What makes them laugh and cry? Why are they so temperamental? Why are they so difficult to get along with? You ask them what's wrong and they say that nothing is wrong – or they go silent and you have no clue what has upset them. What makes them tick?'

The genie ponders for a long minute, and then asks, 'Do you want two lanes or four?'

What a to do!

The worried housewife sprang to the telephone when it rang, and listened with relief to the kindly voice in her ear: 'How are you, darling?' it said. 'What kind of a day are you having?'

'Oh, mother,' said the housewife, breaking into bitter tears, 'I've had such a bad day. The baby won't eat and the washing machine has broken down. I haven't had a chance to do the shopping, and besides I've just sprained my ankle and I have to hobble around. On top of that, the house is a mess and I'm supposed to be having two couples to dinner tonight.'

The mother was shocked and full of sympathy, 'Oh, darling,' she said, 'sit down, relax, and close your eyes. I'll be over in half an hour and I'll do your shopping, clean the house, and cook your dinner for you. I'll feed the baby and I'll call a good repair man I know. He'll be at your house to fix the washing machine promptly. Now stop crying. I'll do everything. In fact, I'll even call George at the office and tell him he ought to come home and help for once.'

'George?' said the housewife. 'Whoever is George?'

'Why, George! Your husband! Is this 234 2166?'

'No, it's 234 2165!'

'Oh, sorry, I must have called the wrong number.'

There was a short pause and then the housewife asked, 'Does this mean you won't be coming over?'

Family fun

Having a family is like having a bowling alley installed in your head.

(Martin Mull)

Food for thought

Isn't it funny how everyone in favour of abortion has already been born?

(Patrick Murray)

Dedicated

I have problems flown in fresh daily wherever I am.

(Richard Lewis)

Shut up!

Until I was thirteen I thought my name was 'Shut Up'.

(Joe Namath)

Super-mum

Somewhere on this earth every ten seconds, a woman gives birth to a child. We must find this woman and stop her at once.

(Sam Levenson)

Romance drained

He kissed me as though he was trying to clear the drains.

(Alida Baxter)

Immaturity

Basically my wife was immature. I'd be home in my bath and she'd come in and sink my boats.

(Woody Allen)

Tough cookie

A woman is like a tea-bag. You can't tell how strong she is until she gets into hot water. (Nancy Reagan)

A big woman

Marry her! Impossible! You mean a part of her; he could not marry her all himself. There is enough of her to furnish wives for a whole parish. You might people a colony with her; or give an assembly with her; or perhaps take your morning's walk round her, always provided there were frequent resting-places, and you were in rude health.

(Sydney Smith)

Temper

People in a temper often say a lot of silly things that they really mean. (Penelope Gilliat)

Love life

My love life is so bad, I'm taking part in the world celibacy championships. I meet the Pope in the semi-finals. (Guy Bellamy)

Ugly

One of my friends who is happily married has a very ugly husband. She met him when a friend sent him over to her house to cure her hiccoughs.

(Phyllis Diller)

In the dark

She could very well pass for forty-three
In the dark with a light behind her.

(W. S. Gilbert)

What diet?

Outside every thin woman is a fat woman trying to get in.

(Katharine Whitehorn)

Motherhood

The joy of motherhood is what a woman feels when all the children are tucked up asleep in bed.

My fault

It was partly my fault when we got divorced – I tended to put my wife under a pedestal.

(Woody Allen)

Ugly baby

I was so ugly when I was born that the doctor slapped my mother three times.

Wise counsel

One Shrove Tuesday a mother was making pancakes for her two sons – Kevin, aged five, and Bryan, aged three – when the boys began arguing about who should get the first one.

Their mother thought it a good opportunity to teach a little moral lesson and explained that if Jesus was sitting where they were, he would say, 'Let my brother have the first pancake. I can wait.'

Quick as a flash, Kevin turned to his younger brother and said, 'Bryan, you be Jesus.'   (J.C.)

Start again

A mother with three troublesome kids was asked whether, if she could turn back the clock, she would choose to have children.

'Oh yes!' she said. 'Just not the same ones.'

Mature reflections

Inside every older person there's a younger person wondering: 'Whatever happened?'

Men and Fathers

Maturing

I told my wife that a husband is like a fine wine – he gets better with age. The next day she locked me in the cellar.

....

Twins

A proud father phoned the local newspaper and excitedly reported the birth of his twins. The girl at the desk didn't quite catch what he had said and asked him:

'Would you repeat that?'

'Not if I can help it!' he replied.

....

What women want in a man

Original list (at age 22): handsome, charming, financially successful, a caring listener, witty, in good shape, dresses with style, appreciates finer things, full of thoughtful surprises.

Revised list (at age 32): nice looking (prefer hair on head), opens car doors, holds chairs, has enough money for a nice dinner, listens more than he talks, laughs at my jokes, carries bags of groceries with ease, owns at least one tie, appreciates a good home-cooked meal, remembers birthdays and anniversaries, seeks romance once a week.

Revised list (at age 42): not too ugly (bald head OK), doesn't drive off until I am in the car, nods head when I am talking, occasionally laughs at my jokes, is in good enough shape to rearrange the furniture, wears a shirt that covers his stomach, shaves most weekends.

Revised list (at age 62): keeps hair in nose and ears trimmed, doesn't scratch or belch in public, doesn't nod off to sleep when I am talking, doesn't retell the same joke too many times, is in good enough shape to get off the couch at weekends, usually wears matching socks and underwear, appreciates a good TV dinner, remembers your name on occasion, shaves some weekends.

Revised list (at age 72): doesn't scare small children, remembers where the bathroom is, only snores lightly when asleep, remembers why he is laughing, is in good enough shape to stand up by himself, usually wears some clothes, likes soft food, remembers where he has left his teeth, remembers that it is the weekend.

Revised list (at age 82): breathing!   (M.M.)

Real pain

Men know nothing of pain. They have never experienced labour, cramps or a bikini wax. (Joan Rivers)

Fatherly advice

I blame my father for telling me about the birds and the bees. I was going steady with a woodpecker for two years.   (Bob Hope)

Parental help

I found parenting so humbling. Every time I gave my kids a helping hand with their homework, their marks went down.

Poor mule

He is like a mule, with neither pride of ancestry nor hope of posterity.

(Robert G. Ingersoll)

Hiding

The phone rings, and, in a whisper, a seven-year-old says, 'Hello.'

'Can I talk to your mother?'

'She's outside,' whispers the little boy.

'Oh, then can I talk to your daddy?'

'No,' whispers the boy, 'he's outside too.'

'Is there anyone else in the house?'

'Yes, my auntie's here.'

'Can I speak to your aunt?'

'No, she's outside too,' says the little boy.

'Is there anybody else around?' asks the caller.

'Yes. The police are here.'

'The police are at your house?'

'Yes,' the little boy whispers. 'They are outside too.'

'Whatever is everybody doing outside?' asks the caller.

'Looking for me.'   (Diana Scott)

....

Great expectations

A child can at least expect that its father be present at the conception.

(Joe Orton)

....

On track

A little boy went with his father to a race-track for the first time.

'What is this strange place, Dad?' he asked.

'This is where people come to race dogs,' replied his father.

After a long, reflective pause, the little boy muttered thoughtfully: 'I bet the dogs win.'

Bragging about Dad

Three small boys in the school playground were bragging about their fathers. One of them boasted, 'My Dad just scribbles a few lines on the back of an envelope and calls it a poem. They give him £50 for it!'

The second boy chipped in: 'That's nothing. My Dad scribbles some words on a piece of paper and calls it a song. They give him £100 for it.'

'Well, my Dad does better than that,' said the third. 'He scribbles down a few words and calls it a sermon – and after that it takes eight people to collect up all the money!'   (J.C.)

Tough guys

Three little boys were boasting about how tough they were.

'I'm so tough,' said the first boy, 'that I can wear out a pair of shoes in a week.'

'Well,' said the second boy, 'I'm so tough, I can wear out a pair of jeans in a day.'

'I can beat that,' said the third boy. 'When I go to see my grandparents, I can wear them out in just an hour.'

A kind thought

I was cutting the lawn on my birthday, when my teenage son came in from playing rugby. Seeing me behind the mower, he exclaimed: 'Oh Dad, you shouldn't be doing this on your birthday.'

I was about to put the mower in his hands when he added: 'You should wait until tomorrow.'

Cat out of the bag

One Sunday we were attending church in our village. The vicar invited the children to the front to give them a short talk before beginning his sermon. He always started with a visual aid and that morning produced a smoke detector. He asked if any children knew what it meant when the detector sounded an alarm. Quickly, my five-year-old raised his hand. 'It means that Daddy is cooking the dinner!'

Get with it, Dad!

An American lad, Kenny, lived in a small community in the deep South. It was in the days when families were beginning to have WCs installed inside their houses.

Kenny's father was not concerned about keeping up with the growing fashion, but Kenny had his own ideas. Their outside privy was on the edge of the river, and he decided to go outside one night and push it into the water, hoping to force his father's hand on the matter.

The next morning his father was very cross and accused him of pushing the privy into the river. Kenny refused to admit it.

Finally his father said, 'Kenny, I want the truth. George Washington grieved his father by cutting down a cherry tree. When he told his father the truth, his father did not punish him. Now Kenny, tell me, did you or did you not push the privy into the river last night?'

With such encouragement, Kenny owned up. 'Yes, I did!'

Whereupon his father took off his belt and gave him a sound beating.

Indignantly the boy reminded his father of what he had said about George Washington's father not beating him for telling the truth.

'Ah yes,' said his father, 'but George Washington's father was not in the cherry tree when he cut it down!'

....

Work out

Remember that by the time you're fifty you will have spent over sixteen years in bed and three years eating.

Keeping fit

Bert was determined to keep fit in his old age, and when he turned sixty he decided to walk five miles every day. He has just reached Adelaide.

Personal Appearance

Slip-up

The bride wore a beautiful gownless evening strap.

....
An exception

I never forget a face, but in your case I'm willing to make an exception. (Groucho Marx)

....
Cash, please

I have always tried to pay my bills with a smile, but they invariably want the money instead.

....
Her great secret

Joan Collins has discovered the secret of eternal middle age.

....
A tall order

Nancy Reagan has had a face lift. Joan Collins uses a fork lift.

Her lovely figure

She has not only kept her lovely figure, but added to it.

(Bob Fosse)

The longest nose

Herr Schnauzer, the world's record holder for the longest nose, has been informed that he no longer qualifies for the trials since his nose measures twelve inches and must now be technically classified as a foot.

Comparisons are odious

Have you ever studied someone of your own age and thought, 'Surely I can't be looking that old?'

I was sitting in the waiting-room for an appointment with my new dentist when I noticed his DDS diploma bearing his full name. Suddenly I remembered a tall, dark-haired, handsome boy by the same name at school some forty years ago. I had a crush on him at the time.

But as soon as I met the dentist, I dismissed any such imaginations. This balding, grey-haired man, with his deeply lined face, was way, way too old to have been my classmate.

After he had checked my teeth, I asked him if he had ever attended Morgan Park High School.

'Yes, I did', he said.

'And what year did you leave?' I asked.

'1959,' he replied. 'Why do you ask?'

'You were in my class!' I exclaimed.

He looked at me closely... and then that ugly, wrinkled old man asked me: 'And what did you teach?'   (J.C.)

....

Starkers

When he criticized the scantiness of her swimsuit, she laughed it off.

....

Silence is golden

Drawing on my fine command of language, I said nothing.

(Robert Benchley)

....

Well built

He must have had a magnificent build before his stomach went in for a career of its own.

(Margot Halsley)

Charmless

William F. Buckley looks and sounds not unlike Hitler – but without the charm.   (Gore Vidal)

Not so flattered

I once had a rose named after me and I was very flattered. But I was not pleased to read the description in the catalogue: no good in bed, but fine up against a wall.   (Eleanor Roosevelt)

Take care!

Watch out when you're getting all you want: only hogs being fattened for the slaughter get all they want.   (Joel Chandler Harris)

Thoughtful

My neighbour asked if he could use my lawnmower, and I told him of course he could, so long as he didn't take it out of my garden.   (Eric Morecambe)

Early retirement

I have so much to do that
I'm going to bed.
     (Robert Benchley)

That helpless feeling

Do you know how helpless you feel if you have a cupful of coffee in your hand and you start to sneeze?

(Jean Kerr)

Sad reflections

A couple were in the bathroom when the wife caught sight of herself in the mirror. She began bemoaning her figure. Her bust had fallen, her stomach was bulging, her posterior was sagging and the veins in her legs were a network of black.

She turned to her husband, expecting some sympathy. 'Oh, darling – can't you find anything to compliment me about?'

'Well,' he said, 'your eyesight seems to be excellent!'

Ear, ear

There was a young man of Devizes,
Whose ears were of all different sizes;
One was quite small,
And of no use at all,
But the other was huge and won prizes.

A lady of Lynn

There was a young lady of Lynn,
Who was so uncommonly thin,
That when she essayed
To drink lemonade,
She slipped through the straw and fell in.

A lady of Flint

There was a young lady of Flint,
Who had an unfortunate squint;
She could scan the whole sky
With her uppermost eye,
While the other was reading small print.

A lady of Spain

There was a young lady of Spain,
Who couldn't go out in the rain;
She'd lent her umbrella
To Queen Isabella,
Who wouldn't return it again.

A sad observation

'I have the body of a man half my age,' said an old athlete. 'Sadly, that man is in terrible shape!'

Children and Growing Up

Nothing new

The children now love luxury; they show disrespect for elders and love chatter in the place of exercise. Children are tyrants, not the servants of their households. They no longer rise when their elders enter the room. They contradict their parents, chatter before company, gobble up dainties at the table, cross their legs and tyrannize their teachers.

(Socrates, 469–399 BC)

A new teacher

Child: 'We had a new teacher and she wanted to know whether I had any brothers or sisters. I told her I was an only child.'
Parent: 'And what did she say?'
Child: 'Thank goodness for that!'

Do babies talk?

Six-year-old Margaret asked her father when their new baby would talk. He told her that it would not be for two years, since little babies don't talk.

'Oh yes they do!' Margaret insisted. 'Even in the Bible they do!'

'What makes you say that?' he asked.

'When the lady read the Bible this morning in church, she definitely said that Job cursed the day he was born!'

What's a baby?

A definition of a baby:
A loud noise at one end and no sense of responsibility at the other.

Any babysitters?

An advert in a local newspaper in the USA: 'Wanted – A babysitter. One dollar per hour – plus fridge benefits.'

Parting words

Babysitter to parents: 'By the way, I promised Mary that if she went to bed quietly, you would buy her a pony in the morning!'

Tact

A woman was once chatting to the mother of a girl. Meaning to be kind, she commented: 'Oh, what a pretty little girl! Is your husband good-looking?'

The singing dad

A doting father used to sing to his little children after he had put them to bed at night, until one day he overheard the five-year-old whispering to his younger brother: 'If you pretend you're asleep, he'll stop soon.'

The blame game

Some people just can't enjoy life. In the first half of their lives they blame their troubles on their parents, and in the second half they blame them on their children.

When I grow up...

Adults are always asking kids what they want to be when they grow up because they are looking for ideas.   (Paula Poundstone)

Old age

Children are a great comfort in one's old age – which one would not reach so quickly if one didn't have children.

Party

The twelve-year-old accompanied his mother to the Communion rail in church to receive a blessing, but as the priest did not know if the boy had been confirmed, he bent down and whispered something in his ear. Then, to the mother's consternation, the priest administered the sacrament. When later his mother asked the boy what had been said, he replied: 'Well, he asked if I was a Conservative and I said Yes.'

Again, please

Auntie, did you feel no pain
Falling from that apple tree?
Would you do it, please, again,
'Cos my friend here didn't see?
(Harry Graham)

Oops!

'Mum, you know that vase you were worried I might break?'

'Yes, what about it?'

'Well, your worries are over.'

Never appreciated

Every luxury was lavished on you –
atheism, breastfeeding,
circumcision.

(Joe Orton)

Divine playmate

A five-year-old surprised his father one day by saying, 'I think I'll go outdoors and play ball with God.'

'How do you play ball with God?' asked the father.

'Oh, it's not hard at all. I just throw the ball up and God throws it back down to me.'

Loud and clear

Johnny, praying in a loud voice before his birthday: 'Dear God, I pray that I will get a new bicycle for my birthday.'

His brother: 'What are you shouting for? God isn't deaf.'
Johnny: 'I know, but Granny is.'

Too much to swallow

Sunday school teacher: 'What do we learn from the story of Jonah and the whale?'
Ten-year-old Jane: 'People make whales sick.'

Dog lick

The little boy started to cry after a large and friendly dog bounded up to him and licked his hands and face.

'What is it?' asked his mother. 'Did he bite you?'

'No,' sobbed the child, 'but he tasted me!'

Off to the zoo

Mother: 'Today I want you to take your brother Eddie to the zoo.'
Roy: 'Not me. If they want him they'll have to come and get him.'

Fishy reply

'Now, children,' said the Sunday school teacher, 'I have told you the story of Jonah and the big fish. Willie, please tell me what this story teaches us.'

Willie, the bright-eyed son of the vicar, replied: 'It teaches that you can't keep a good man down.'

The things they say!

A six-year-old complained to her mother that she had a pain in her tummy.

The mother replied: 'My dear, your stomach's empty. When you have got something in it you'll feel better.'

Later the vicar called but said he could not stay as he had a terrible headache.

'Don't worry,' said the little girl. 'You'll feel better when you have got something in it!'

What is it?

The class were on a nature walk when Tommy asked Miss Brown, his teacher, 'What has eight legs, six eyes, yellow spots and purple spikes down its back?'

'I've never heard of such a thing,' Miss Brown replied.

'Well,' said Tommy, 'there's one on your collar now.'

So delighted

A little boy desperately wanted a role in the school's play. The teacher was going to tell the class that morning who had which parts. His mother was very worried about his feelings if he was overlooked.

She went to fetch him from school in the afternoon and was greeted by an excited infant running towards her calling out: 'Mummy, Mummy, I've been picked!'

'How wonderful, darling. What have you been picked to do?'

'I've been picked to clap and cheer!'

Self-discipline

A man in a supermarket was pushing a trolley that contained, among other things, a screaming baby. As the man proceeded along the aisles, he kept repeating softly, 'Keep calm, George. Don't get excited, George. Don't yell, George.'

A lady watched with admiration and then said, 'You are certainly to be commended for your patience in trying to quiet little George.'

'Lady,' he declared, 'I'm George!'

Still standing

A father repeatedly told his little boy to sit down on the back seat of the car, but he remained standing until eventually, exasperated, the father physically sat the boy down.

The little boy grimaced and muttered, 'I may be sitting down on the outside, but I'm still standing up on the inside!'

Suspicious

Mother: 'What are you doing at the fridge, Willie?

William: 'Fighting temptation, Mother.'

Get the name right

A young student was trying to earn some money over the summer vacation. He knocked on the door of a wealthy neighbour and asked if there was anything he could do for cash.

'Yes,' the man replied. 'You can paint the porch. The brushes and paint are in the garage.'

Three hours later, the student reported back. 'Well, it's all painted, but I have to tell you that it's not a Porsche; it's a Ferrari.'

Potential fortune

Two young women were taking a stroll across a farm when a large green frog leapt up before them, calling out: 'Please, girls, one of you kiss me, and I will be turned into a handsome prince!'

Immediately one of them grabbed the frog and popped it into her handbag.

'Aren't you going to help him turn back into a handsome prince?' said her friend, in surprise.

'No! Princes are two a penny. A talking frog has potential!'

Refund

A teenager, buying a dress from a boutique, enquired first if it would be all right to bring it back for a refund if her parents liked it!

Growing up

A teenager is grown up when he thinks it is more important to pass an examination than to pass the car ahead.

Hollow legs

Meal-time is when the youngsters continue eating but sit down.

Whose brains?

Father: 'Don't you think our son gets all his brains from me?'

Mother: 'Probably. I still have all of mine.'

No need to whisper

When Jenny finally brought her boyfriend home, her parents were hopeful that he might turn out to be Mr Right. But having got to know him a bit, they took Jenny aside for a chat.

'He's not exactly a young man, is he?' Mum whispered to her daughter. 'He's fat, he's bald and he's pretty old, isn't he?'

'Mum, there's no need to whisper,' said Jenny, 'he's stone deaf too.'

Prudent advice

A young man entered a jewellery store and bought an expensive engagement ring. The jeweller asked him, 'What name do you wish to be engraved in it?'

'From John to Elaine,' whispered the embarrassed young man.

The jeweller looked from the ring to the young man and smiled. 'Take my advice, young fellow,' he said. 'Have it inscribed simply *From John*.'

How rude!

Mother: 'How could you be so rude as to call your sister stupid? Now just tell her you're sorry.'

Boy: 'Sis, I'm sorry you're stupid!'

Father and Son

Father: 'Son, do you realize that when Abraham Lincoln was your age, he was already studying hard to be a lawyer?'

Son: 'Right, Dad, and when he was your age, he was already President of the United States!'

Any mother's nightmare

A mother entered her daughter's bedroom and saw a letter on the bed. She opened it with trembling hand and an awful premonition. She read the letter through to the end. It ran:

Dear Mum,

It is with great regret and sorrow that I'm telling you that I have eloped with my new boyfriend. I have found real passion and he is so nice, even with all his piercings and tattoos, and I love riding on the back of his big motorcycle with my hair blowing freely in the wind.

But it's not only that, Mum. I'm pregnant and Dave said that we will be very happy together in his trailer in the woods. He wants to have many more children with me, and that's one of my dreams.

I've learnt that marijuana doesn't hurt anyone and we'll be growing it for us and his friends, who are providing us with all the cocaine and ecstasy we may want.

In the meantime we'll pray for science to find a cure for AIDS for Dave to get better. He deserves it.

Don't worry, Mum, I'm fifteen years old now and I know how to take care of myself. Some day I'll visit you again and you can get to know the grandchildren.

Your daughter
Jane

PS: Mum, it's not true. I'm next door at Sandy's. I just wanted to help you get things in perspective before you read my report card which is in my desk drawer... I love you!

Trying to run away

I know a teenage girl who has been trying to run away from home for a year – but every time she gets to the front door, the phone rings.

No great expectations

A six-year-old was explaining to his grandmother that he was never going to get married. But his grandmother suggested that he might change his mind when he was older. 'Most people do,' she said.

'All right,' he replied, 'I might get married but don't expect me to kiss her!'

Life after marbles

My grandsons were playing marbles when a pretty little girl walked by. 'I'll tell you what,' said the older boy to his younger brother. 'When I stop hating girls, that's the one I'm going to stop hating first.'

Lost in the game

My brother Jack was great at playing hide-and-seek. He was so good at it that we haven't seen him since 1972.

Let me out!

A young man walking the beach in Florida kicked a bottle in the sand and noticed something moving inside. When he opened it, a genie jumped out.

'Thank you, thank you!' said the genie. 'I've been corked up in that bottle for over a hundred years. Now I want to reward you with three wishes.'

The young man thought for a moment and said, 'Well, if you really mean it, I've always wanted a Porsche! What can you do about that?'

The genie simply waved his wand, and a shiny red Porsche appeared out of thin air.

'What next?' asked the genie.

'Oh, that's more than enough!' said the young man.

'No!' insisted the genie, 'I said you can have three wishes. What next?'

'All right. I'd like a beach-hut right here.'

A simple wave of the genie's wand, and there was a huge beach-hut.

'And now your last wish?'

'Oh, this is more than enough!' said the young man.

'No,' said the genie, 'I insist. You still have one wish left!'

'Well, perhaps you can help me one more time. I've never been able to find a beautiful woman who liked me enough to marry me. Could you please make me irresistible to women?'

The genie thought for a moment, waved his wand – and turned him into a box of chocolates!

Will you marry me?

A young bachelor was desperately pleading with a beautiful blonde to marry him, but with absolutely no success.

'Why won't you marry me?' he asked. 'Is there somebody else?'

She replied, with a desperate sigh, 'There's got to be!'

Teen tact

When your Dad is cross and asks you, 'Do I *look* stupid?' – don't answer.

Don't tell Mum

Never tell Mum her diet is not working.

Peace and quiet

Never allow your three-year-old brother in the same room as your homework.

How to get what you want

If you want a kitten,
start by asking for a horse.

How not to make do

Don't use felt-tip markers
as lipstick.

Growing Old

Don't mention it

You know you are getting older when the only thing you want for your birthday is not to be reminded of it.

(Jeff Rovin)

....

As old as possible

If a man has to grow old, he might as well grow as old as he can.

(Catherine Hall)

....

Talking to myself

'I say, old fellow, who is old Humberton talking to?
  'He's talking to himself!'
  'Then why is he shouting?'
  'He's deaf!'

....

We, the survivors
(for those born before 1940)

We were born before television; before penicillin, polio shots, frozen foods, Xerox, contact lenses, videos and the Pill. We were before radar, credit cards, split atoms, laser beams and ball-point pens; before dishwashers, tumble-driers, electric blankets, air conditioners, drip-dry clothes...and before man walked on the moon.

We got married first and then lived together (how quaint can you be?). We thought 'fast food' was what you ate in Lent, a 'Big Mac' was an over-sized raincoat, and 'crumpet' was what we had for tea. We existed before house-husbands and computer-dating, and 'sheltered accommodation' was where you waited for a bus.

We were before day-care centres, group homes and disposable nappies. We never heard of FM radios, tape-decks, artificial hearts, word proces-sors, or of young men wearing earrings. For us 'time sharing' meant togetherness, a 'chip' was a piece of wood or a fried potato, 'hardware' meant nuts and bolts, and 'software' was not a word.

Before 1940 'made in Japan' meant junk, the term 'making out' referred to how you did in your exams, 'stud' was something that fastened a collar to a shirt, and 'going all the way' meant staying on a double-decker bus to the terminus.

In our day, cigarette smoking was 'fashionable', 'grass' was mown, 'coke' was kept in a coal-house, a 'joint' was a piece of meat you ate on Sundays, and 'pot' was something you cooked in. 'Rock music' was a fond mother's lullaby. 'Eldorado' was an ice-cream, a 'gay person' was the life and soul of the party, while 'aids' just meant beauty treat-ment or help for someone in trouble.

We who were born before 1940 must be a hardy bunch, when you think of the way in which the world has changed, and the adjustments we have had to make. No wonder there is a generation gap today. But, by the grace of God we have survived!   (Printed on a tea towel)

A letter from Grandma

The other day I went up to the local Christian book-store and saw a 'Honk if you love Jesus' bumper-sticker. I was feeling particularly sassy that day because I had just come from a thrilling choir performance followed by a thunderous prayer meeting, so I bought the sticker and put it on my bumper.

Boy, I'm glad I did! What an uplifting experience followed! I was stopped at a red light at a busy inter-section, just lost in thought about the Lord and how good he is, and I didn't notice that the light had changed. It is a good thing someone else loves Jesus because if he hadn't honked, I'd never have noticed! I found that LOTS of people love Jesus!

Why, while I was sitting there, the guy behind me started honking like crazy, and then he leaned out of his window and screamed, 'For the love of GOD! GO! GO!' What an exuberant cheerleader he was for Jesus!

Everyone started honking! I just leaned out of my window and started waving and smiling at all these loving people. I even honked my horn a few times to share in the love!

There must have been a man from Florida back there because I heard him yelling something about a 'sunny beach'. I saw another guy waving in a funny way with only his middle finger stuck up in the air. Then I asked my teenage grandson in the back seat what that meant. He said it was probably a Hawaiian good luck sign or something.

Well, I've never met anyone from Hawaii, so I leaned out the window and gave him the good luck sign back. My grandson burst out laughing. Why, even he was enjoying this religious experience!

A couple of people were so caught up in the joy of the moment that they got out of their cars and started walking towards me. I bet they wanted to pray or ask what church I attended, but this was when I noticed the light had changed.

So, I waved to all my brothers and sisters, and drove on through the intersection. I noticed I was the only car that got through the intersection before the light changed again, and I felt kind of sad that I had to leave them after all the love we had shared, so I slowed the car down, leaned out of the window, and gave them all the Hawaiian good luck sign one last time as I drove away.

Praise the Lord for such wonderful folks!

Love,

Grandma (M.M.)

So grateful

The old woman had been going on a bit, so when she asked, 'Have I ever told you about my lovely grandchildren?' one of the listeners replied, 'No – and may I say how truly grateful we are about that!'

If Only

If I had known I was going to live so long, I would have taken better care of myself.

(Leon Eldred)

Who was it?

A guy lent me a book on memory training last week. I want to return it but I can't remember his name.

Past worrying

A 102-year-old woman was asked whether she had any worries. 'No, I haven't,' she replied. 'Not since my youngest son, aged 76, went into an old folk's home.'

A useful tip

When I meet a man whose name I cannot remember, I give myself two minutes, then if it is a hopeless case I always say, 'And how is the old complaint?' (Benjamin Disraeli)

Two topics

Poor old Lord Mortlake only had two topics of conversation, his gout and his wife. I never could quite make out which of the two he was talking about.

(Oscar Wilde)

All in the Name

The town drunk received an unexpected inheritance and was finally able to fulfil his lifelong dream of building his own houseboat and retiring. He called the boat *Cirrhosis of the River*.

An honest confession

I have never killed a man, but I have read many obituaries with a lot of pleasure. (Clarence Darrow)

A bad day

'I'm very brave generally,' he went on in a low voice: 'only today I happen to have a headache.'

(Lewis Carroll)

A new way out?

I don't believe in dying. It's been done. I'm working on a new exit. Besides, I can't die now – I'm booked.

(George Burns)

Concentration

The realisation that one is to be hanged in the morning concentrates the mind wonderfully.

(Samuel Johnson)

Are You Sure?

The reason why so many people showed up at Louis B. Mayer's funeral was to make sure he was dead.

(Samuel Goldwyn)

Natural law

There is only one immutable law in life – in a gentleman's toilet, incoming traffic has the right of way.

(Hugh Leonard)

No flowers, please

At my age flowers scare me.

(George Burns)

Jumbo consultant

I have a memory like an elephant.
In fact elephants often consult me.

(Noel Coward)

Stronger now

A reporter was interviewing a man who was believed to be the oldest resident in town.

'May I ask you how old you are?' the newsman inquired.

'I just turned a hundred this week,' the old man proudly replied.

'Great! Do you suppose you'll see another hundred?' the reporter asked playfully.

'Well,' said the man thoughtfully, 'I'm stronger now than when I started the first one hundred!'

And we really mean it

They say such nice things about people at their funerals that it makes me sad to realize that I'm going to miss mine by just a few days.

(Garrison Keillor)

Grave humour

As he was lowering the body into its last resting-place, the respected grave-digger suddenly collapsed and died, which event cast a gloom over the entire proceedings.   (Bernard Falck)

Millstone

In the midst of life we are in debt.

(Ethel Mumford)

Future plans?

A young minister asked an elderly parishioner what plans he had for the future. The old man replied, shaking his head, 'At my age I don't even buy green bananas.'

What else?

You know you are getting old when you stoop to tie your shoes and wonder what else you can do while you're down there.   (George Burns)

How old?

A little boy asked an elderly man how old he was.

The old man replied, 'I'm eighty-five.'

'Gosh,' said the little boy, 'you're old enough to be dead!'

Grandpa's generosity

I'm very proud of my gold pocket-watch. My grandfather, on his death-bed, sold me this watch.

(Woody Allen)

Chamber of Horrors

I took my mother-in-law to Madame Tussaud's Chamber of Horrors and one of the attendants said, 'Keep her moving, we're stock-taking.'

(Les Dawson)

Julius Caesar

Teacher: 'Have you ever heard of Julius Caesar?'
Pupil: 'Yes, sir.'
Teacher: 'What do you think he would be doing now, if he were alive?'
Pupil: 'Drawing an old-age pension.'

An old Londoner

Tourist: 'Have you lived here all your life?'
Old Londoner: 'Not yet.'

A good deed

Three Boy Scouts told their Scoutmaster they had done their 'good deed' for the day.

'Well boys, what did you do?' asked the Scoutmaster.

'We helped an old lady across the street on our way here,' the boys chimed out in unison.

'And did it take all three of you to do that?' asked the Scoutmaster suspiciously.

'Yes it did,' chorused the boys. Then the smallest one added, 'She didn't want to go.'

Peanut horror

An old lady on a group outing kept offering the driver a handful of peanuts to eat. The third time she came forward, he asked her why she was so generous to him.

'Well,' she said, 'it would be a pity to waste them. My husband and I both have poor teethbut we can still enjoy sucking the chocolate off them first.'

(J.W.)

Many qualms

King David and King Solomon lived
    merry, merry lives,
With many, many concubines, and many,
    many wives.
But when old age came over them, with
    many, many qualms,
King Solomon wrote the Proverbs and
    King David wrote the Psalms.

The ages of man

The seven ages of man: spills, drills, thrills, bills, ills, pills, wills.

(Richard J. Needham)

The ages of man (again)

The four ages of man: lager, Aga,
Saga and ga-ga.

Anecdotage

As we grow older, our bodies grow shorter and our
anecdotes get longer. (Robert Quillen)

Aches and pains

Increasing twinges in the hinges.
(Dick Lyth)

At that age

I'm at the age when my back goes
out more than I do.
(Phyllis Diller)

Peer pressure

There is a great advantage in living
to be 105 – no peer pressure!

Aching feet

Patient: 'My right foot hurts.'

Doctor: 'It's just old age.'

Patient: 'How come my left foot doesn't hurt? It's just as old.'

Famous ancestor

John: 'I hear one of your ancestors fell at Waterloo.'

Paul: 'Yes – he was pushed off platform 3.'

Confused theology

Did you hear about the agnostic, dyslexic insomniac who lay awake at night wondering, 'Is there a Dog?'

History exam

People nowadays treat the Ten Commandments like a history exam – they attempt only three.

Different types

There are three types of people: those who make things happen; those who watch things happen; and those who haven't a clue what's happening!

Granny on the Pill

I heard about a grandmother who went on the Pill. She didn't want any more grandchildren!

He so old and she so young

A 70-year-old multi-millionaire married a beautiful young shapely blonde. When asked how he had managed such a successful scoop, he explained that he had lied and told her that he was 90!

Right beside you

With his wife at his bedside, a dying man was reflecting on his life. 'Honey,' he said to her, 'you have always been there for me. You were there when I lost my job… when I was involved in that terrible road accident – you were right by my side.

'And that time when I fell off the roof, you were there to call the ambulance. During those years of dark depression you stood by me, and when the business went bankrupt. And now, as I lie at death's door, you are right beside me, just as you have always been.'

There was a long silent pause for further tearful reflection. Then the old man glanced up at his wife and said, 'Elsie, I have just realized something. You're bad luck!'

Fifty Years of Marriage

Luigi was down at the pub celebrating his marriage of fifty years. Friends gathered to congratulate him and to buy him a few drinks. Marvelling, they asked him the secret of his long-lasting union. He gave them all the usual reasons.

Then one of them asked about any really special thing he might have done to please his wife during that time.

'Yes,' he said, 'after twenty years of marriage I took my wife to Italy.'

'And are you thinking of anything special for this fiftieth anniversary?'

'Well...I was thinking I might fetch her back.'

Spin over sin

The Smith family in America were proud of their family history, having a forefather who had arrived from England aboard the *Mayflower*. Former generations had included senators, famous scientists and well-known plutocrats.

The Smith family hired an excellent genealogist to write up their ancestry as a legacy for future generations of Smiths. The only embarrassment was that one of their forefathers had been executed in the electric chair.

The genealogist was asked to write up this shameful detail in a sensitive way. He thought it over and suggested that it might be best to mention it as follows:

> Great-uncle Jack had once occupied a chair of applied electronics at an important government institution. He had been attached to this position by the strongest of ties until the time of his death, which came as a great shock.

....

Family tree

Every time I look up my family tree, they throw nuts down!

....

The missing wife

A man drove into an M1 service centre to fill up his petrol tank. His wife popped into the restroom. The man paid for his petrol and absent-mindedly drove off without her. About ten miles down the M1 he was stopped by police.

'Excuse me, Sir,' said the police officer, 'but are you aware that you left your wife behind at the last service centre?'

'Oh! Thank goodness for that,' he said. 'I thought I'd gone deaf!'

Hearing aids

1. The vicar was enquiring how his elderly parishioner was getting on with her new hearing aid. 'Oh, splendidly, Vicar!' she replied. 'I can hear everything that is being said around me now. And I've already removed three relatives from my will!'

2. A vicar suggested to an elderly lady that it might be a good idea for her to get a free hearing aid on the NHS. 'Thank you,' she said, 'but I think at ninety-one I've heard enough!'

3. A man was regaling his doctor about his marvellous new hearing aid which, he claimed, had revolutionized his life.

'What kind is it?' enquired the doctor with genuine curiosity.

Glancing down at his watch, the man replied: 'Two thirty!'

Dying, Funerals and the Afterlife

The Hereafter

Old Jack, the village atheist, had made a remarkable recovery from a stroke. When the Vicar was visiting later he thought it was time to suggest to Jack that he should start thinking about the serious challenges of life after death. He chose his words carefully and tactfully:

'Now, Jack, don't you think it's about time you gave serious thought to the hereafter?'

Old Jack thought for a moment and then replied: 'But Vicar, I do that frequently.'

'Really, Jack?' enquired the delighted Vicar. 'How long have you been thinking about the hereafter?'

'Well, it's like this, Vicar. 'Since I come 'ome, every time I go into another room I thinks to meself: "Now, whatever did I come hereafter?"'

Foot work

The Vicar was conducting the last rites for Joe Biggs, one of the most popular members of his congregation.

He had been visiting Joe in hospital and found him in bed, unable to speak. Breathing had obviously become an acute problem. Believing that prayer was called for, the Vicar drew nearer and placed his hands on Joe's head.

At this point Joe clearly indicated that he had something urgent he needed to tell the priest. Groping for a pen at his bedside, he scribbled a brief note but as he passed it to the Vicar, he fell back on his pillow, apparently dead. With all the rush and scramble for medical assistance that followed, the Vicar simply slipped the note into his pocket. Alas! No medical assistance could revive poor Joe.

During the funeral the Vicar was telling everyone just how much Joe would be missed when he suddenly recalled the note, crumpled and still unread, in his pocket. Believing the last words of such a well-loved man would be timely, he fished it out and read it to the gathered mourners. The message was simple: 'Vicar – your foot is on my oxy...'

....
Big Question

Priest to Paddy: 'Do you want to go to heaven?'

Paddy: 'No, Father.'

Shocked priest: 'But surely you must want to go to heaven when you die!'

Paddy: 'Oh yes, Father, when I die. I thought you were getting a party together now!'

Revelation

My wife converted me to religion. I never believed in hell until I married her.

I'm still here

The reports of my death have been greatly exaggerated.

(Mark Twain)

Over the hill

When you are over the hill you tend to repeat yourself. When you are over the hill you tend to repeat yourself.

(Ron Chichowicz)

The old school

If capital punishment was good enough for my father, it's good enough for me. (Victor Moore)

A good holiday

An old man went to the west coast for a month's holiday. He hadn't been back more than two days when he suddenly died. Two of his friends were standing by his open coffin.

'Doesn't he look wonderful?' said one.

'He certainly does,' said the other. 'That month's holiday must have done him the world of good!'

First Funeral

A five-year-old boy attended his first funeral with his family. Asked afterwards what he thought of it, he replied: 'Well, she was already dead when we got there.'

The atheist's tomb

An inscription on the tomb of an atheist:

HERE LIES AN ATHEIST.
ALL DRESSED UP AND NO PLACE TO GO.

Dying Wish

A dying man had worked all his life and made a fortune, but he was a real Scrooge when it came to giving any money away. He left his wife clear instructions that she was to bury all his money with him when he died so that he would have the use of it in the afterlife.

After he died and had been placed in his coffin, the undertaker was just closing it up when his widow popped a box in beside the body. The casket was then locked and wheeled away.

A friend watching the proceedings turned to her and said: 'Surely you would not be fool enough to bury all that money with your deceased husband!'

'Well, I promised my husband,' said the loyal wife, 'that he would be buried with his money.'

'You mean to tell me that you are burying him with all that money!'

'I certainly am,' she replied. 'I got it all together, put it into my account, and placed the cheque in the coffin. If he can cash it, he can spend it!'

(M.B.)

Tribute to a scoundrel

A rich man lost his brother. They were both well known as ruthless scoundrels. The surviving brother approached a vicar and promised that, if he would officiate at the funeral and call his brother a 'saint' in his eulogy, he would pay all the expenses for a large church extension being planned. The vicar was not a man to compromise but badly wanted to build the extension, so he agreed.

The service went along without a hitch, and the vicar maintained his integrity. The widow sat wondering how the vicar would ever get round to calling her deceased husband a saint. When it came to his address, he openly admitted that this man had a terrible reputation in the community, but compared to his brother, *he was a saint*.

Undertakers

1. My friend, the undertaker, is the last person on earth to let me down.

2. I have nothing against undertakers personally. It's just that I wouldn't want one to bury my sister.

(Jessica Mitford)

Which one?

There were two brothers, one of whom died. On bumping into the survivor, an elderly lady asked, 'Was it you who died, or was it your brother?'

The class system

Class distinction is only temporary. All men are cremated equal.

Cremation

My uncle Fred died of asbestosis – it took six months to cremate the poor man.

Is he really dead?

He was a great patriot, a humanitarian, a loyal friend – provided, of course, he really is dead.

(Voltaire)

Signing off

Did you hear about the undertaker who closes all his letters with the words, 'Eventually yours'?

Choosing your words

It's not always easy to say the right thing on the spur of the moment. We can sympathize with the chap who met an old friend after many years. He asked:

'How's your wife?'

'She's in heaven.'

'Oh, I'm so sorry.'

Realizing this was not quite what he wanted to say, he stammered: 'I mean, I'm glad.' That seemed even worse, so he blurted, 'Well, what I really mean is, I'm surprised!'

A good shot

Blown his brains out, you say? He must have been an incredibly good shot! (Noel Coward)

Post mortem

I don't mind dying; the trouble is,
you feel so stiff the next day.

(George Axlerod)

Grave thoughts

First old man greeting very old friend: 'Hello,
George, I thought you were dead.'
George, 'No, I'm not dead.'
First old man: 'If you're not dead, whose funeral did
I go to in February?'

Tit for tat

If you don't go to other men's funerals, they won't come to yours.

(Clarence S. Day)

Who is it?

Every time you see a church
Just pay a little visit.
So when at last you're carried in
The Lord won't say, 'Who is it?'

Epitaphs

1. In this grave here do I lie,
   Back to back my wife and I.
   When the last trump the air shall fill,
   If she gets up, I'll just lie still.

2. Oh Lord, she is thin...
   *(It's said that this epitaph appears at the
   head of a Tasmanian tombstone. The 'e' is
   on the reverse side of the headstone – the
   mason ran out of space!)*

3. Here lies James Burke,
   A decent man entirely.
   We bought this tombstone second-hand –
   And his name's not Burke, it's Reilly.

4. Down the lanes of memory
   The lights are never dim,
   Until the stars forget to shine
   We shall remember... her.
   (From a Lancashire newspaper)

For sale

Full-length undertaker's coat, left
shoulder slightly worn, £6.
(Advertisement in the *Chester Observer*)

Try these!

An after-dinner speaker arrived for his engagement, having forgotten his false teeth. He turned to the man next to him and confessed, 'I have forgotten my teeth.'

'No problem,' said the man, and passed him a set which he just pulled from his pocket. 'Try these!'

The speaker popped them into his mouth but found them too loose.

'I have another pair,' said the man. 'Try these!'

The speaker tried them. 'Too tight!' he said, shaking his head.

'Never mind!' said the man. 'I have one more pair. Try them!'

This time they fitted perfectly.

After the speaker had made his speech, he turned to thank his helpful fellow guest.

'I want to thank you for coming to my aid. Where is your office? I've been looking for a good dentist.'

The man replied, 'I'm no dentist. I'm an under-taker!'   (M.B.)

Dead end

My luck is so bad that if I bought a cemetery, people would stop dying.   (Ed Furgol)

Getting there

'Heaven is not reached in a single bound,' says the poet. 'It may be on a busy street corner.'

Life in heaven

To live above with saints we love,
Oh! That will be grace and glory!
To live below with saints we know,
Well, that's a different story!

Marriage in heaven?

Just days before their wedding, a couple were killed in a car crash. When they got to heaven they asked St Peter whether it was possible for them to get married, as their sudden death had robbed them of the opportunity. St Peter promised to find out.

After five years of investigation, St Peter returned and told them they could be married. The prospective bride had used those five years to get to know her husband better and by then she was reflecting on a marriage to him for eternity. She felt she needed to check with St Peter whether, in the event of the marriage not working out, they would be able to get a divorce.

At this, St Peter became very cross with her. 'It took me all of five years to find a minister up here!' he complained. 'Now, imagine the problems I'll have trying to find a lawyer!'

Values

Sharp young man at the Pearly Gates, to St Peter: 'You must be bored with your job, showing people in year after year, century after century?'

St Peter: 'You must remember, here in heaven things are measured differently. A million years are but as a minute; a million pounds are but a penny.'

Sharp young man, after a moment's reflection: 'Could you loan me a million pounds, holy saint?'

St Peter: 'Certainly – just wait a minute!'

Any suggestions?

A newcomer at the Pearly Gates was surprised to find a suggestion box so near the entrance. He asked a long-time resident what it was for.

'Well,' said the seasoned resident, 'it's because some people are never happy unless they are complaining.'

A points system?

A man died and went to the Pearly Gates, where St Peter greeted him.

'Please let me in!' said the man.

'Here's how it works,' said St Peter. 'You need 100 points to make it to heaven. Tell me all the good things you have done and I'll tell you how many points you chalk up for each item, depending on how good they were. When you have reached 100 points you're in.'

'Okay,' the man said. 'I was married to the same woman for fifty years and never cheated on her, even in my heart.'

'That's wonderful!' said St Peter. 'That's worth three points!'

'Only three points?' said the man, slightly miffed. 'Well, I attended church all my life and supported the ministry with my tithes and service.'

'Tremendous!' said St Peter. 'That's worth another point.'

'Only one point?' groaned the man, looking worried. 'Ah, I started a soup kitchen in my town and helped in a shelter for the homeless.'

'That great!' said St Peter. 'That's two more points.'

'Just two points for that?!' the man cried desperately. 'At this rate I'll never get to heaven except by the grace of God!'

'Bingo!' said St Peter. 'That's 100 points! Come on in.' (J.C., from *Mikey's Funnies*)

Voting for St Peter

Voter: 'Why, I wouldn't vote for you if you were St Peter himself!'

Candidate: 'If I were St Peter, you couldn't vote for me – you wouldn't be in my constituency.'

Heaven and hell

Heaven is an English policeman, a French cook, a German engineer, an Italian lover and everything organized by the Swiss.

Hell is an English cook, a French engineer, a German policeman, a Swiss lover and everything organised by the Italians.   (John Elliot)

Money in the bag

An elderly gentleman put ten pence into the collection plate at church one Sunday.

'What happens to all this money?' he asked the young priest standing by the plate.

'It goes to the Lord,' answered the priest.

'Oh, well,' said the old man, removing his ten pence from the plate, 'I'm seventy-five years old. I'm bound to see the Lord before you, and I can give it to him personally.'

Money and Giving

Let-downs

A lot of people become pessimists
from financing optimists.

(C. T. Jones)

....

The poor

Always remember the poor –
it costs nothing.

(Josh Billings)

....

Selected

Dear *Reader's Digest*, we hardly know each other, yet
I have been selected from so many millions to enter
your free contest in which I may win £25,000. You
have made me very happy.   (Miles Kington)

....

Missing credit card

I haven't reported my missing credit card to the
police because whoever stole it is spending less
than my wife.   (Ilie Nastase)

Borrowing

You should always live within your income, even if you have to borrow to do so.

(Josh Billings)

Happiness

What's the use of happiness? It can't buy you money.

(Henry Youngman)

Income

I'm living so far beyond my income that we may almost be said to be living apart. (E. E. Cummings)

Forgive us our debts!

If there's anyone to whom I owe money, I am prepared to forget it if they are. (Errol Flynn)

A striking formula

My formula for success is rise early, work late, and strike oil.

(Paul Getty)

A cheerful giver

Hoping to develop his son's character, a father once gave him fifty pence and ten pence as he was leaving for Sunday school. 'Now, Bill, you put whichever one you want on the offering plate,' he said.

When the boy returned, his father asked which coin he had given. Bill answered, 'Well, just before they sent around the plate the preacher said, "The Lord loves a cheerful giver," and I knew I could give the ten pence a lot more cheerfully than I could the fifty, so I gave the ten.'

A good investment

There was a man,
Men thought him mad.
The more he gave,
The more he had.

Charities

A solicitor representing a well-known charity made an appeal to the actor W. C. Fields.

Fields replied that he would have to talk with his own solicitor.

'And what will you do if he says yes?' asked the solicitor.

'I'll get another solicitor,' said Fields.

Wisdom

He is no fool who gives up what he cannot keep to gain what he can never lose. (Jim Elliot)

Happy spending

Money can't buy you happiness – unless you spend it on somebody else.

Times are hard

Take my silver and my gold,
Not a mite would I withhold.
But as times are rather hard,
Please accept my Barclaycard.

Kindness to war veterans

A vicar was walking along the high street when he saw a man in an army greatcoat standing outside one of the main stores selling boxes of matches from a tray tied by a string around his neck. On the front of the tray hung an emotional notice: 'Please help a Veteran of the Falklands War.'

The vicar, being of a kindly disposition and wanting to help one of the lads who had braved the harsh conditions of war and climate in that far-off region of Antarctica, gave the soldier a most generous donation.

The soldier, overcome by such kindness, touched his cap and said in a choking voice: 'Muchas gracias, señor.'

Farmers, Farm-hands and Hoboes

Off My Property

One sunny afternoon a farmer, armed with a bucket, was making his way across his farm to fetch some water from his reservoir.

He discovered on arrival that a number of girls were skinny-dipping there. He told them that they were trespassing and must leave. They all said they would go, but not until he had left.

'No problem,' he said. 'I've only come here to feed the alligator!'

....
Free access

The following notice was nailed to the gate of a farmer's field:

> The farmer who owns this field allows ramblers to cross it for free – but the bull charges.

Who was the stranger?

A stranger approached a sheep farmer and asked him, 'If I can guess the number of sheep on your farm, may I have one?'

Thinking this was improbable, the farmer agreed.

'Two thousand, three hundred and seven,' said the stranger, and the farmer, reluctantly, confirmed that he was right.

The man casually selected an animal, slung it over his shoulder and turned to leave.

'Just a minute,' said the farmer. 'If I can guess your occupation, can I have that animal back?'

'Fair deal!' replied the stranger.

'You are a government bureaucrat,' responded the farmer with a grin.

'How on earth did you work that out?' asked the stranger in astonishment.

'Well,' replied the farmer, 'if you'll just put that dog down, I'll tell you.'

A daily constitutional

1st man: 'Every day my dog and I go for a tramp in the woods.'

2nd man: 'Does the dog enjoy it?'

1st man: 'Yes, but the tramp's getting a bit fed up!'

What's it worth?

'Say, vicar, would you give me £1 for a sandwich?'
  'I don't know. Let me see the sandwich!'

No such thing as a free lunch

A disreputable tramp goes into a restaurant and orders food. The waiter refuses, saying, 'I don't think you have the money to pay for it.'

'You're right,' says the tramp. 'I don't have the money, but if I show you something you've never seen before, will you let me have a hamburger?'

'Okay – it's a deal,' says the waiter.

The tramp reaches into his coat pocket and produces a hamster. He puts it onto the counter and it scampers off to the end of the room, leaps up onto a piano keyboard and starts playing Gershwin songs.

'That's a truly amazing hamster!' gasps the waiter, and gives him a hamburger.

The tramp scoffs it down and asks for another.

'Only if you show me another miracle,' said the waiter.

The tramp reaches down into his pocket and pulls out a frog which he also places on the counter. The frog immediately begins to sing. It has a brilliant voice.

At this point a client from the other side of the room runs over and offers the tramp £300 for the frog.

'Done!' said the tramp, and, taking the money, hands over the frog. Immediately the new owner runs out of the restaurant with his latest purchase.

'You idiot,' said the waiter to the tramp, 'you've sold a singing frog for a paltry £300!'

'Not to worry,' said the tramp, shoving the banknotes into one pocket and the hamster into the other. 'This hamster is also a wonderful ventriloquist.'

A midnight guest

A couple heard their doorbell ring in the middle of the night. The husband went down to open the door and was greeted by a stranger asking for a push.

Seeing the drizzle outside, the householder said he was sorry and closed the door.

When he was back in bed, his wife asked him who was at the door. He told her the story and confessed what he had done.

She said: 'Darling, how could you do that? Don't you remember when we were first married, someone helped us out in the middle of the night?'

Conscience-stricken, the husband got up and dressed and went down again. He opened the door and called out: 'Are you still there?'

'Yes!' came the reply out of the dark.

'Do you still need a push?'

'Yes!' the distant voice responded.

'Whereabouts are you, then?' the householder enquired.

'Over here by the swing.'

Donkey's Dinner

An old man was standing by his donkey, giving the animal its lunch by attaching a feeding bag to its head.

A passer-by started to mock him. 'You'll never do it! You'll never do it!'

'Never do what?' queried the old man, looking puzzled.

'You'll never get that great big animal into that tiny little bag.'

Driving, Flying and Exploring

Pig-headed

A middle-aged couple were driving along the road one night when a traffic cop stopped them.

'You were travelling at 90 m.p.h.,' said the policeman.

'Ridiculous!' said the husband at the driving wheel. 'It was only 60.'

The cop insisted on 90 and the driver was getting angry, when the wife intervened to calm the situation down. 'Don't argue with him, officer. He's always pig-headed when he's had a few drinks.'

....
The reason why

'Don't you know that you can't sell second-hand cars without a licence?' said the police officer.

'Thanks. I knew I wasn't selling any cars, but I didn't know the reason!'

A wife's alarm

An elderly man was driving along the highway when his car-phone rang. It was his wife telling him to be careful, as she had just heard on the news that there was a car driving the wrong way up the M1.

'Oh my goodness!' her husband suddenly gasped in horror. 'It's not just one – there's dozens of them!'

Red lights ahead

Two elderly ladies were out driving in a large car. Both could hardly see over the dashboard. As they were cruising along they came to a crossroads. The lights were red but they just went on. The passenger thought to herself: 'I must be losing my mind. I swear we just went through a red light.'

A few minutes later they came to another set of lights, and although they were red they sailed right through again. This time the passenger was certain the lights had been red but was concerned that she might have been mistaken again. She was getting nervous and decided to pay very close attention to the road and to see what was really going on.

At the next crossroads, sure enough, the lights were definitely red, but once again they went right through them. This time she spoke up.

'Did you know we have just been through three sets of red lights? You could have killed us.'

The little old lady beside her looked up and said: 'Oh, am I meant to be driving?'

Other drivers

Have you ever noticed, when you are driving, that the man going slower than you is an idiot and the man going faster than you is a maniac?

A scared passenger

Nervous passenger: 'Don't drive so fast around the corners – it frightens me.'

Driver: 'Do as I do – shut your eyes when we come to one.'

What a cheek!

I was just getting into my old banger in town last night when a policeman asked if I had reported the accident.

Alcohol

Ten per cent of all accidents are caused by drivers affected by alcohol. This is another way of saying that 90 per cent of accidents are caused by non-drinkers.

Road safety

Keep death off the roads –
drive on the pavement.

Collision

A collision is what happens when two motorists go after the same pedestrian.   (Bob Newhart)

Gear

The policeman was taking down details from a woman he had stopped for speeding.

'What gear were you in?' asked the cop.

'An apricot-yellow two-piece with a chartreuse picture-hat,' she replied.

Watch out!

A careful driver is one who looks in both directions when he passes a red light.(Ralph Marterie)

An old wreck

I drove to the garage for an oil change. The mechanic lifted up the bonnet and suggested, 'If I were you, sir, I'd keep the oil and change the car.'

Wearing glasses

After checking the driver's licence, the highway patrolman said, 'It says here you're supposed to be wearing glasses.'

'But officer, I have contacts.'

'I don't care who you know, you are still breaking the law.'

Stalled at the lights

The stalled car sat dead still at the traffic lights as they went to red, to red and yellow, to green, to yellow, and back to red.

Finally a police motorcyclist drew up and said, 'Pardon me, sir, but don't we have any colour to suit you?'

Inherited inhibitions

My ancestors wandered lost in the wilderness for forty years, because even in biblical times men would not stop to ask for directions.

(Elayne Boosler)

One-way street

A policeman stopped a man driving the wrong way on a one-way street. 'Didn't you see the arrow?' he demanded.

'Arrow? Honest, Officer, I didn't even see the Indians.'

Who's driving?

A man with four teenage daughters and a rather bossy wife confessed: 'I don't drive any longer. I just sit behind the wheel.'

French Cabby

A French taxi-cab driver had Sir Arthur Conan Doyle as a passenger. He took him from the station to a hotel, and when he received his fare, he said, '*Merci*, Monsieur Conan Doyle.'

'Why, how do you know my name?' asked Sir Arthur.

'Well, sir,' replied the taxi man, 'I have seen in the papers that you were coming from the south of France to Paris. Your general appearance told me that you were English. Your hair was clearly last cut by a barber in the south of France. I put these indications together and guessed at once that it was you.'

'That's very remarkable,' replied Sir Arthur. 'You have no other evidence to go upon?'

'Well,' hesitated the man, 'there was also the fact that your name was on your luggage.'

....

Flying

There is nothing safer than flying – it's crashing that is dangerous.

(Theo Cowan)

....

Out of fuel

Bad weather forced a plane to keep on circling over the airfield. Finally, the pilot announced over the PA system: 'Ladies and gentlemen, I have some bad news and some good news. The bad news is that we are running out of fuel. The good news is that I am parachuting down to get help.'

....

Parting blessing

A pastor was seeing a member of his congregation off at the airport and left her with his blessing: 'May God and your luggage go with you.'

Rude passenger

A luggage handler was very patient with a traveller who was continuously rude to him as he coped with his luggage. A fellow traveller asked the handler how he could tolerate such abuse.

'It's easy,' said the young man. 'That guy is heading for New York. I'm sending his baggage to Buenos Aires!'

Lost luggage

Explorers in South America are said to have discovered several lost airstrips. They also reported having found a mountain of ancient lost luggage.

Scientific Theory

The scientific theory I like best is that the rings of Saturn are composed entirely of lost airline luggage.

(Mark Russell)

British pride

Never make excuses, never let them see you bleed, and never get separated from your baggage.

(Wesley Price)

Parachute problems

A parachutist was hurtling towards the ground, his parachute having failed to open. As he fumbled in panic with his straps, he was amazed to pass a man ascending heavenwards rapidly.

'Do you know anything about parachutes?' he shouted out desperately.

'No!' the man replied. 'Do you know anything about gas ovens?'

A good deal

A farmer and his wife went to a fair. The farmer was fascinated by the daredevil aeroplane rides, but balked at the £10 tickets.

'Let's make a deal,' said the pilot. 'If you and your wife can ride without making a single sound, I won't charge you anything. Otherwise you pay the ten pounds.'

'Good deal!' said the farmer.

So off they flew for a series of aerial acrobatics. On return, before alighting, the pilot turned and said, 'If I hadn't been there, I would never have believed it. You never made a sound!'

'It wasn't easy, either,' said the farmer. 'I almost said something when my wife fell out.'

Questions, questions

He: 'Excuse me, stewardess. How high is this plane?'
She: 'About 30,000 feet.'
He: 'Oh. And how wide is it?'

Do something, Vicar!

An airliner flew into a violent thunderstorm and was soon swaying and bumping around in the sky.

One very nervous lady happened to be sitting next to a clergyman and turned to him for comfort.

'Can't you do something?' she demanded forcefully.

'I'm sorry, ma'am,' said the reverend gently. 'I'm in sales, not management.'

Engine failure

Norman Vincent Peale was once on an aeroplane when the Captain's voice came over the intercom:

'We need to inform you that one of our engines has shut down, but the other three will enable us to complete our journey all right.' Then he added, 'To reassure any of you who might be worried, let me tell you that we have four Methodist bishops on board today.'

A woman beside Peale called a stewardess over and said, 'With respect to the Captain, could you please tell him I'd be far happier if there were three bishops and four engines?'

Blowing in the wind

I knew immediately when I had reached the North Pole, because in one step the north wind became a south wind. (Robert Peary)

Seasons, Sermons, Bishops and Church

Some good advice

Go to church on Sunday now and avoid the Christmas rush.

....

A valuable gift

'Thanks for the harmonica you gave me for Christmas,' said little Joshua to his uncle. 'It's the best present I ever had.'

'That's good,' said his uncle. 'Do you know how to play it?'

'Oh, I don't play it,' he replied. 'My Mum gives me 50p a day not to play it during daylight and my Dad gives me £5 a week not to play it at night.'

(J.C.)

....

Gift-list

A little boy was handing his gift-list to his parents to email to Santa Claus before Christmas, but there was one gift not included in the list because, he said, he wanted to talk directly to his grandparents about it first!

Last-minute order

'Dear Sandy Klaus: I wanna put in a new order quick, as I just found all the things which I asked you for under the spare room bed.'

Father's play time

Send the children to bed early on Christmas Eve. It gives their fathers more time to play with their toys.

The three stages of man

There are three stages of man: he believes in Santa Claus; he does not believe in Santa Claus; he is Santa Claus. (Bob Phillips)

Three Wise Women

Q: Can you imagine what would have happened had it been Three Wise Women who came to the stable instead of Three Wise Men?

A: They would have asked for directions, arrived promptly, cleaned the stable thoroughly, made a suitable meal for the parents and brought some practical gifts!

Christmas cards

It doesn't matter how many Christmas cards you may send each year – the first you receive will be from someone you've forgotten.

No speech-maker

So many people start with the words, 'I am not really a speech-maker.' Then they spend the next half hour proving it.

Delusional

I was an atheist until I realized I was God.

A good sermon

A good sermon should be like a woman's skirt: short enough to rouse interest, but long enough to cover the essentials.

(Ronald Knox)

Lapsed

He was of the faith chiefly in the sense that the church he currently did not attend was Catholic.

(Kingsley Amis)

And God said...

As God once said, and
I think rightly...

(Attributed to Margaret Thatcher)

Sleepless sheep

The lion and the lamb shall lie down together, *but the lamb won't get much sleep.*

Interruptions

I don't like being interrupted when I am praying. There's something about putting God on hold...

(Joan Rivers)

Did the Pope know?

Pompeii was destroyed by an overflow of saliva from the Vatican.　　(K. F. Banner)

Fence-sitting

Some people say there is a God; others say there is no God. The truth probably lies somewhere in between.　　(W. B. Yeats)

Graffiti

'God is dead' – Nietzsche.
'Nietzsche is dead' – God.

Bathroom theology

'Mum, does God use our bathroom?'

'No! Why on earth would he do that?'

'Because Dad was standing outside the door this morning asking, "My God! Are you still in there?"'

Looking for loopholes

I have spent a lot of time searching through the Bible for loopholes. (W. C. Fields)

Love thy neighbour

The Bible tells us to love our neighbours, and also to love our enemies – probably because they are generally the same people. (G. K. Chesterton)

Closing their eyes

When the missionaries came to Africa they had the Bible and we had the land. They said, 'Let us pray.' We closed our eyes. When we opened them, we had the Bible and they had the land.

(Desmond Tutu)

Gob-smacked

Answering the door to two people who introduced themselves by saying, 'Good morning, we're Jehovah's Witnesses', the white-bearded man replied, 'Good, I'm Jehovah. How are we doing?'

(Rachel Dutton)

Say that again?

Jesus: 'Who do you say that I am?'

The disciples: 'You are the eschatological manifestation of the ground of our being, the kerygma in which we find the ultimate meaning of our interpersonal relationships.'

Jesus: 'What?'

Quick exit

Some scholars were discussing the reason for Jesus' fairly sudden ascension after the Great Commission. They concluded that Jesus made a quick exit to avoid the debate.

Sounds reasonable

Three men of God were asked the same question: 'When does life begin?'

The Catholic priest said: 'At the moment of conception.'

The Anglican clergyman said: 'When the child is born.'

The Rabbi said: 'When the children are married, the dog has died and the mortgage has been paid off.'

Dead dogma

Sorry, but my karma just
ran over your dogma.

Mistaken identity

The parish priest was a welcome visitor for short-sighted Mrs Flannegan. 'I always enjoy our priest's visits,' she remarked appreciatively to her daughter after he had left.

'But that wasn't the priest,' said her daughter, 'that was the doctor.'

'Oh, was it?' exclaimed Mrs Flannegan with relief. 'I thought Father O'Reilly was getting a bit familiar!'

Putting it off

Procrastination is my sin,
It brings me naught but sorrow.
I know that I should stop it,
In fact, I will – tomorrow!

(Gloria Pitzer)

Nuns' confessions

Hearing nuns' confessions is like being stoned to death with popcorn. (Father J. Sheen)

Many meanings

The word *good* has many meanings. For example, if a man were to shoot his grandmother at a range of five hundred yards, I should call him a good shot, but not necessarily a good man. (G. K. Chesterton)

Gratitude

Thank God I'm an atheist.

(Luis Buñuel)

Wistful comment

Why do 'born again' people so often make you wish they had never been born the first time?

(Katherine Whitehorn)

How long, O Lord?

Few sinners are saved after the first twenty minutes of a sermon. (Mark Twain)

Escape from the nunnery

Monica Baldwin's book *I Leapt Over the Wall* strengthened my desire not to become a nun.

(Noel Coward)

Sermon secret

The secret of a good sermon is to have a good beginning and a good ending and having the two as close together as possible.   (George Burns)

Interference

Things have come to a pretty pass when religion is allowed to invade the sphere of private life.

(W. L. Melbourne)

Churchmen

There is a species of person called a 'Modern Churchman' who draws the full salary of a beneficed clergyman and need not commit himself to any religious belief.   (Evelyn Waugh)

Jewish tradition

I was raised in the Jewish tradition, taught never to marry a Gentile woman or shave on a Saturday night and, most especially, never to shave a Gentile woman on a Saturday night.   (Woody Allen)

Don't bank on it

Jesus was born on a bank holiday and died on a bank holiday. We can therefore assume that when he returns again it will also be on a bank holiday.

(P. G. Johnson)

Straight down the line

I must believe in the Apostolic Succession, there being no other way of accounting for the descent of the Bishop of Exeter from Judas Iscariot.

(Sydney Smith)

Be warned

I have noticed again and again since I have been in the church that lay interest in ecclesiastical matters is often a prelude to insanity.

(Evelyn Waugh)

Preach to the sick

There is not the least use in preaching to anyone unless you chance to catch them ill.

(Sydney Smith)

Dodgy editor

I am increasingly convinced that the *Church Times* is now edited by the Devil in person.

(Bishop Gore)

Papal misdeeds

The most scandalous charges against the Pope were suppressed. His holiness was accused only of piracy, rape, murder, sodomy and incest. (Edward Gibbon)

Ignore the clergy

My dear child, you must believe in God in spite of what the clergy tell you. (Margot Asquith)

Long sermons

What he lacked in depth as a preacher he made up for in length. (Mark Twain)

Retirement

I resigned because of illness and fatigue. The congregation were sick and tired of me.   (A. Vicar)

Catastrophic congregation

The sermon was a great success, but the congregation was a disaster.   (Anon)

Staying in the lead

It is said that Norfolk folk are not known for their adaptability. A Bishop of Norwich was told that the only way to lead the people of his diocese was to find out first which way they were going and then walk in front of them.

Memory gaffs

A former Bishop of Gloucester had a defective memory and on one celebrated occasion was walking round a garden party at his home greeting the clergy.

'My dear fellow,' he said to one clergyman, 'how lovely to see you here today; and how is your dear wife?'

The clergyman, rather surprised, replied, 'She's dead, my Lord. Don't you remember, you wrote me a very helpful letter at the time?'

'I am so sorry,' the Bishop exclaimed. 'Do please forgive me.' He moved on.

Later that afternoon the Bishop came across the same man again. 'Hello,' he exclaimed, 'so good to have you with us. And how is your dear wife?'

'Still dead, my Lord,' said the priest. 'Still dead!'

....
Overheard

The Bishop had preached at Harvest Festival and as he stood at the door, people were very complimentary about his sermon. 'Splendid,' said one. 'Thank you for the wonderful message,' said another – and so it went on.

However, one rather shabbily dressed man took the Bishop's hand and said, 'Pathetic,' before moving out.

The compliments started again, but after a few minutes the strange man was back in the queue. This time he said to the Bishop, 'Very, very boring,' and again went through the door.

The pattern repeated itself yet again. This time the message was, 'Hope it will be a long time before we see you again.' Soon everyone had gone except the churchwarden.

'Who was that strange man?' asked the Bishop. 'He said very peculiar things.'

'Don't worry about him,' came the reply. 'He's a bit simple and he just wanders round repeating what he hears other people saying.'

Episcopal French

A Bishop of London was seated next to the French Ambassador. During the meal a fly settled on the tablecloth. Although the conversation had been in English, the Bishop was keen to show off his knowledge of French.

'*Le mouche*,' he said, airily.

After a brief glance, the Ambassador corrected him, '*LA mouche.*'

The Bishop looked back at the insect, observing it from this angle and that. Finally he exclaimed, 'I must say you've got remarkably good eyesight!'

Episcopal help

The sudden illness of an incumbent necessitated a plea for help to the Bishop. In the emergency, the Bishop himself came and took the service. Afterwards, two very over-awed Churchwardens felt that they must express their thanks to the Bishop. This they did in the following words: 'My Lord, we greatly appreciate your ready kindness in coming to us. A poorer preacher would have suited us all right but we couldn't find one.'

Episcopal confusion

A Victorian Archbishop, taking his last Confirmation, placed his two hands on a bald head and muttered, 'I declare this stone well and truly laid.'

(Source – his successor)

Episcopal satisfaction

Henry Montgomery Campbell, Bishop of London, hated meetings of all kinds. 'Waste of time,' he would snort.

On one occasion, he went into a meeting of the Board of Finance intoning: 'We brought nothing into this meeting and it's certain we can carry nothing out.'

But then he brightened up a bit. 'Must admit I've had a good day today,' he said. 'Really enjoyed it – I've been out of the diocese to bury a vicar.'

Episcopal bruising

When Walter Frere was Bishop of Truro, a vicar invited him to stay the night after a Confirmation. Before supper, Frere was walking down a dimly lit passage in the vicarage when the vicar's wife, coming up from behind, gave him a clout over the ear, with the remark: 'That'll teach you to ask the Bishop to stay when we've nothing in the house.'

Episcopal embarrassment

When William Greer was retiring from the See of Manchester, he said that although he would miss many things, there was one aspect of his life which would be improved by laying down the burden of office. 'For years,' he confessed, 'I have found it embarrassing to sign hotel registers with the names "William Manchester" and "Marigold Greer".'

A quick-thinking bishop

A Bishop of Carlisle was terminating an interview with a very difficult woman of the diocese who had come to Rose Castle once again to lodge a complaint. They were in the hall, getting round to the final handshake, when the Bishop's wife called downstairs, 'Has that stupid woman finally gone, dear?'

Quick as a flash, the Bishop replied, 'Yes, my love, she went ages ago. I'm with Mrs Robinson just now.'

A good excuse

I remember Bishop Victor Whitsey asking me to attend a meeting. It was on a Saturday afternoon about six weeks away, and I remember saying to him, 'I'm terribly sorry, my Lord, I cannot go. I have a funeral.'

He said, 'A funeral! What do you mean? It's in six weeks' time.'

'I know,' I said. 'I am hoping to bury fifteen Englishmen at Twickenham.'   (A Welsh priest)

....
Episcopal advice

A Bishop of Manchester once gave his bachelor curates some advice about finding the right kind of wife. He said, 'Find a woman who is pretty, prudent and with private means, and make sure these are in the reverse order!'

....
Twisted words

Archbishop Geoffrey Fisher used to enjoy telling true stories concerning the press. One was about a visit to the United States aboard the *Queen Elizabeth*. As soon as the ship docked, a swarm of reporters arrived to interview him. He prided himself on his ability to parry awkward questions.

Within seconds, one was flung at him: 'Archbishop, do you intend to visit the night-clubs in New York?'

With a wry smile, the Archbishop countered with, 'Why, are there any night-clubs in New York?'

His self-congratulations lasted only until the morning papers arrived. One of them carried the headline, 'ARCHBISHOP WANTS TO KNOW.' Beneath the headline the report began:

The very first question asked by the Archbishop of Canterbury on his disembarkation at New York yesterday was, 'Are there any night-clubs in New York?'

....
National Service

In the grim days of 1939 and 1940, notices about National Service were posted up in Employment Exchanges throughout Great Britain. The official orders stated that 'All persons in the above age-groups are required to register for National Service except lunatics, the blind and Ministers of Religion.' Much in common, evidently.

....
BBC warning

The BBC issued a strong warning because of the widespread storms and advised anyone who had to go out to wear something white so that they would be clearly seen by motorists. One vicar had to go to visit a sick parishioner, so he put on his white surplice over his raincoat. Alas, he was knocked down by a snow-plough!

....
A wife's advice

The doctor and the parson were standing with the wife beside a dying old man's bed.

'I'm afraid he's gone,' said the priest.

'Yes, he has,' said the doctor.

'No, I ain't,' murmured the patient, feebly sitting up.

'Lie down, dear,' said his wife. 'The doctor and the parson know best.'

New brooms

Parishioner: 'I have nothing but praise for the new vicar.'

Sidesman: 'I noticed that when I came round with the plate last Sunday.'

Was he pushed?

Our vicar left three months ago, so we gave him a little momentum from the parish.

Fringe benefits

There was once a poor curate who was bemoaning his impecunious state in the hearing of his vicar. 'Never mind,' came the rejoinder, 'the fringe benefits are out of this world.'

Liturgical daughter

The Vicar's small daughter was seen and heard burying a dead bird in the garden: 'In the Name of the Father, and of the Son, and into the hole he goes. Amen.'

The road to recovery

The Vicar had been in hospital for several weeks, undergoing routine surgery, and at last he was able to ask his churchwardens to let his parishioners know he was on the road to recovery.

The next day people were startled to find the following announcement on the church noticeboard: 'God is good. The Vicar is better.'

Retirement

Clerical retirement doesn't reduce us all to cleriatrics!

A fair exchange

The Vicar of a small village received an invitation to dine one evening with the Squire. As the village was sparsely lit, the Vicar took a lantern to light him through the dark lanes. He had a very enjoyable time indeed and returned home safe and sound.

Next morning, he received a note from the Squire: 'Dear Vicar, if you will kindly return the parrot in its cage, you can have your lantern back.'

He never knew

The doctor went to see her, but the Vicar
    didn't go:
But the doctor had been sent for, and the
    Vicar didn't know.
The doctor got rewarded with a handsome
    little cheque,
But the Vicar for not knowing simply got it
    in the neck.

From a school essay

… and when the marauders landed on the coast, the villagers would run to the top of the hill and set fire to the deacon…

Diocesan discipline

A curate was transferred to a diocese whose bishop was renowned for being a very strict disciplinarian. His parish priest greeted him with the words: 'Welcome to the Cruel See…'

Cricket crazy

An old clergyman was so besotted with cricket that he occasionally said 'Over' instead of 'Amen'. On one celebrated occasion, having just read out a Bible passage, he proclaimed, 'Here endeth the second innings.'

After he had a new parish hall built, he had signs put on the doors: one said 'Out' and the other 'Not out'.

He even liked to preach on the game, and his favourite texts were:

- Peter stood up with the eleven and was bold (Acts 2:14).
- I caught you by guile (2 Corinthians 12:16).
- … drinking in the pavilions (1 Kings 20:12).

The old Verger

The Vicar announced one Sunday that he was leaving the parish to take up another post elsewhere in the Diocese. He was quite touched afterwards to find the old Verger sitting at the back of the church with his head in his hands and his eyes full of tears.

The Vicar tried to reassure him. 'Don't get upset,' he said, 'there will soon be another Vicar here and I've no doubt he will be a lot better than me.'

'Oh no, he won't,' said the old man. 'The last Vicar said that when he went, and it wasn't true.'

From a church service sheet

Solo: Death, where is thy sting?
Hymn: Search me, O God.

Commandments

'Our church is very liberal: four commandments and six do-the-best-you-cans.'

The classic joke about canons

The bigger the gun, the bigger the bore.

Prayer time

A little boy's prayers: 'Dear God – same as last night – Amen.'

A question about prayer

Little Jimmy had finished his nightly prayer and asked me what prayers were. I told him they were little messages to God.

Quickly he nodded, 'Oh, yes! And we send them at night to get the cheaper rates.'

Printed in Great Britain
by Amazon